MARK

BRINGING THE BIBLE TO LIFE

Genesis, by John H. Walton, Janet Nygren, and Karen H. Jobes
   (12 sessions)

Esther, by Karen H. Jobes and Janet Nygren
   (8 sessions)

Psalms, by Gerald Wilson, Janet Nygren, and Karen H. Jobes
   (10 sessions) — summer 2010

Daniel, by Tremper Longman III, Janet Nygren, and Karen H. Jobes
   (10 sessions)

Mark, by David E. Garland, Karen-Lee Thorp, and Karen H. Jobes
   (12 sessions)

John, by Gary M. Burge, Karen Lee-Thorp, and Karen H. Jobes
   (12 sessions)

Acts, by Ajith Fernando, Karen Lee-Thorp, and Karen H. Jobes
   (12 sessions) — summer 2010

Romans, by Douglas J. Moo, Karen Lee-Thorp, and Karen H. Jobes
   (12 sessions)

Galatians, by Scot McKnight, Karen Lee-Thorp, and Karen H. Jobes
   (6 sessions)

Ephesians, by Klyne Snodgrass, Karen Lee-Thorp, and Karen H. Jobes
   (6 sessions)

Hebrews, by George H. Guthrie, Janet Nygren, and Karen H. Jobes
   (8 sessions)

Revelation, by Craig S. Keener, Janet Nygren, and Karen H. Jobes
   (10 sessions) — summer 2010

BRINGING
THE
BIBLE
TO LIFE

MARK

Gospel of the Servant King

David E. Garland
and Karen Lee-Thorp

Karen H. Jobes, Series Editor

ZONDERVAN.com/
AUTHORTRACKER
follow your favorite authors

We want to hear from you. Please send your comments about this
book to us in care of zreview@zondervan.com. Thank you.

ZONDERVAN

Mark
Copyright © 2010 by David E. Garland, Karen Lee-Thorp, and Karen H. Jobes

Requests for information should be addressed to:

Zondervan, Grand Rapids, Michigan 49530

ISBN 978-0-310-32043-2

Cover design: Tammy Johnson
Cover and interior photography: Gettyimages, BiblePlaces, The Bridgeman Art Library
Interior design: Michelle Espinoza

Printed in the United States of America

CONTENTS

SERIES PREFACE

Have you ever been in a small-group Bible study where the leader read a passage from the Bible and then invited the members of the group to share what the passage meant to them? God wants to speak to each person individually through the Bible, but such an approach to a group study can often be a frustrating and shallow experience for both leader and participants. And while the same passage can speak in various ways into people's lives, the meat of the Word is found in what the biblical writer intended to say about God and our relationship to him. The Bringing the Bible to Life series is for those who are ready to move from a surface reading of the Bible into a deeper understanding of God's Word.

But the Bible, though perhaps familiar, was written in ancient languages and in times quite different from our own, so most readers need a bit more help getting to a deeper understanding of its message. A study that begins and ends with what a passage "means to me" leaves the meaning of the passage unanchored and adrift in the thoughts – and perhaps the misunderstanding – of the reader. But who has time to delve into the history, language, cultures, and theology of the Bible? That's the work of biblical scholars who spend their lives researching, teaching, and writing about the ancient Scriptures. The need is to get the fruit of all that research into the hands of those in small-group Bible studies.

Zondervan's NIV Application Commentary (NIVAC) series was written to bring the best of evangelical biblical scholarship to those who want to know *both* the historical meaning of the biblical text *and* its contemporary significance. This companion series, Bringing the Bible to Life, is intended to bring that material into small-group studies in an easy-to-use format. Pastors, Christian education teachers, and small-group leaders whether in church, campus, or home settings will find these guides to be an enriching resource.

Each guide in the series provides an introduction to the biblical book that concisely summarizes the background information needed to better understand the original historical context. Six to twelve sessions per guide, with each session consisting of eleven to thirteen discussion questions, allow a focused study that moves beyond superficial Bible reading. Relevant excerpts from the corresponding NIVAC commentary provide easy access into additional material for those interested in going even deeper. A closing section in each session assists the group in responding to God's Word together or individually. Guidance for leading each session is included, making the task of small-group leadership more manageable for busy lives.

If you want to move from the biblical text to contemporary life on solid ground, this series has been written for you.

Karen H. Jobes, PhD
Gerald F. Hawthorne Professor of
New Testament Greek and Exegesis
Wheaton College and Graduate School

OF SPECIAL NOTE

Your experience with and understanding of the gospel of Mark can be deepened and enriched by referring to the volume on which it is based: *The NIV Application Commentary: Mark* by David E. Garland, published by Zondervan in 1996.

INTRODUCTION

CONFIDENCE TESTED

To be a Christian in Rome in AD 64 was to face economic ruin, "vicious gossip and hostility"[1] from your neighbors, even arrest and a horrific death. Ten of the city's fourteen wards were mere ashes after a disastrous fire, and people with formerly stable jobs were destitute. There were rumors that Emperor Nero had secretly set the fire in order to renovate part of the city. To save himself from rebellion, Nero blamed Christian arsonists. He had Christians rounded up, and if they refused to renounce Christ and denounce other Christians, they were burnt, torn apart by dogs, or crucified.

To stay committed to Christ in such a time, you had to be 100 percent confident in what the eyewitnesses to Jesus' life, death, and resurrection said about him. But at that time there was no New Testament. Instead, Peter and the other apostles were telling their memories orally. They had been young men when they had followed Jesus some thirty-five years earlier, but now they were old and several had died. Peter was in Rome, and it became clear that someone needed to write down Peter's memories before he died or was arrested.

This someone left himself anonymous in the manuscript he wrote (the desire to be famous apparently didn't cross his mind). A writer two generations later tells us his name was Mark. He may have been the John Mark mentioned in Acts, Colossians, Philemon, and 2 Timothy, but Marcus/Marcos was a common name, and what mattered wasn't the author's identity but the reliability of the record.

THE BEGINNING

The title Mark gives to his book says a lot: "The beginning of the good news about Jesus the Messiah" (1:1). Not the whole of the good news, but the beginning. Mark's tale launches abruptly, hurtles forward, and ends just as abruptly with bewildered women fleeing from Jesus' empty tomb. Obviously that isn't the end of the story—the other gospels tell us how Jesus appeared to people after his resurrection, and Acts recounts what the apostles did in the years after that. But Mark leaves this to other writers, because he knows that the good news about Jesus is still ongoing, the end has yet to be written, and his job is to record how it all started.

"The Greek word *arche* ('beginning') can also indicate the basis or foundation of something."[2] Jesus' life, death, and resurrection are not just the starting point, but also the foundation, of the good news that Christians proclaim.

Mark writes for people who are asking, "Is Jesus truly the Messiah, the deliverer, the King foretold in the Hebrew Scriptures?" To Christians risking brutal death at the hands of the state he shows a Messiah who says "Follow me" before his own brutal death. To the frightened and afflicted citizens of Rome he shows Jesus calming storms and healing afflictions. This is the beginning of the story of a King who could have escaped suffering, but who instead had the courage to lead the way through it to the other side.

A GOSPEL

In modern English, a gospel ("good news," Greek: *euangelion*) is a type of literature invented by Mark. But in Mark's day, the verb *euangelizo* was associated with Roman emperors, whose toadies competed to pen the most over-the-top flattery about the emperor's birth and accomplishments. Rome's subjects received these proclamations of imperial news with public applause and private eye-rolling. One inscription about Caesar Augustus reads, "The birthday of the god was for the world the beginning of the gospel concerning him...."[3] Mark appropriates this phrasing for his news about Jesus to create a contrast between the kingdom of God and the kingdom of Caesar, inviting his readers to choose their allegiance (1:1, 14, 15; 8:35; 10:29; 13:10; 14:9). Mark is saying, in effect, that while the emperor may claim to be the source of blessing for all mankind, Jesus actually is. (This is the kind of thing that could have gotten Mark fed to dogs.)

MESSIAH

Mark tells us up front that Jesus is the Messiah, or Christ (which means "anointed one"). Like us, his readers have heard the term often and think they know what it means. But Mark's gospel is full of characters who "use the title but have no idea of what it means for Jesus of Nazareth to be the Christ. As the story unfolds, it becomes plain that one must throw out all preconceptions of what *Christ* means. Only after Jesus' death and resurrection can one understand the momentous nature of the news that he is God's Christ."[4]

The Hebrew word *Messiah* (or in Greek, *Christ*) was a Jewish term for one whom the prophets said would come from God to liberate Israel. Notions of the Messiah conjured images of a military leader overthrowing the Romans, ruling with justice from Jerusalem, restoring Israel to prosperity, and even subduing neighboring nations. By that definition it was impossible that a man whom the Romans had executed as a criminal could be the Messiah. A "crucified Messiah was an oxymoron, like calling a prisoner on death row, 'Mr. President.'"[5] Mark means us to feel "the scandal of Jesus as the Christ ... who exposes our false hopes and selfish expectations."[6]

"We today are little different from first-century Jews and the disciples in wanting a Messiah who does our bidding, wins our wars, destroys our enemies, and exalts us.... The Messiah we meet in Mark is a rude awakening to those who are more interested in themselves and in ensuring their personal salvation and entrance to eternal life (10:17) than in God or the fate of God's world."[7]

Something remarkable has begun. In a dangerous world, a scandalous Messiah calls us. Will we follow?

NOTES

1. David E. Garland, *The NIV Application Commentary: Mark* (Grand Rapids: Zondervan, 1996), 28.
2. Garland, 18–19.

3. P. Stuhlmacher, *Das paulinische Evangelium I. Vorgeschichte* (Forschungen zur Religion und Literatur des Alten und Neuen Testaments 95; Göttingen: Vandenhoeck & Ruprecht, 1968), 186.
4. Garland, 21.
5. Garland, 23.
6. Ibid.
7. Garland, 25.

THE MESSIAH ARRIVES

Mark 1:1–45

In his book *The Image*, Daniel Boorstin points out the distinction between heroes and celebrities. A hero is someone who does something good for others, often at great personal cost. An example of a hero is "Father Damien, who, in 1870, went to serve the lepers banished to the island of Molokai [in the Hawaiian Islands]. He lived with the corrupted bodies, the stench, the rats and flies, and no running water to fulfill what he said was his priestly duty — to let them know that God has not forsaken them. He himself died a leper, having contracted the disease of those he served."[1]

By contrast, celebrities are well known for their produced and packaged fame, not for their deeds. An example is the pop star whose personal life is followed by millions even though she isn't a great singer, let alone a great human being. Our society is obsessed with celebrities but skeptical of heroes.

Yet as Mark launches his gospel, he takes pains to show that neither Jesus nor his forerunner John have the slightest interest in being celebrities. Fame, they know, is empty, and there is a wide gulf between being a fan and being a disciple.

MARK'S PROLOGUE[2]

Read Mark 1:1 – 13.

The central question of Mark's gospel is, "Who is Jesus?" Throughout most of the drama, even those devoted to God are in the dark about who Jesus is. But in these opening scenes, Mark lets us glimpse from a heavenly vantage point who Jesus is and why he has come.

John the Baptist dresses like the prophet Elijah (cf. 2 Kings 1:8) and demands that Jews undergo the same rite of cleansing from sin that non-Jews undergo when they convert to Judaism.

1. What can we learn from John the Baptist about who Jesus is and why he is coming (1:2 – 8)?

2. Mark 1:2 – 3 interconnects three Old Testament passages, and Mark suggests a double meaning. How is John the messenger who prepares the way for Jesus?

How is Jesus the One sent to prepare the way for us to follow?

John is powerful, and the Coming One will be more powerful (1:7) — but not in the usual sense of money and military force. John is nobody, except that he proclaims God's mighty will. The Coming One will display his power in doing God's will — by serving, suffering, dying.

3. What power have you sought to have or use? Power to do what? Power by what means?

    How is that "way" of power like or unlike the way of power in which Jesus walks?

The Coming One arrives not from the sophisticated capital city, but from backwoods Galilee. We get a private glimpse over his shoulder as he sees the heavens torn (1:10). "God is now in our midst and on the loose. The hope of Isaiah, 'Oh, that you would rend the heavens and come down, that the mountains would tremble before you!' (Isa. 64:1) has come to pass."[3]

4. The crowds don't hear the voice that speaks from heaven in 1:11, and they go on about their business. But we readers hear it. What do you think Mark wants us to learn about Jesus from overhearing these private words between Father and Son?

How do you think Mark wants us to respond?

GOING
DEEPER
No sooner has the Father secretly declared his Son to be the promised king than the Spirit leads him out to the wilderness. For Jews, the wilderness/desert was more than just a place on the margins of civilization.... [I]t marked the place of beginnings. It was the region where God led the people out and from which they crossed over Jordan and seized the land promised to them. It was the place to which God allured the people to win them back (Hos. 2:14).... [It] was also considered to be "the staging ground for Yahweh's future victory over the power of evil."[4]

5. Mark tells us none of the details of Jesus' temptation in the wilderness that we get from Matthew and Luke. He only says it was dangerous — wrestling with Satan and wild animals nearby — but Jesus was assisted by angels (1:13). What do you think Mark is trying to tell us about Jesus here?

JESUS LAUNCHES HIS MINISTRY IN GALILEE[5]

Read Mark 1:14–45.

"John is more than a town crier who precedes Jesus. He is Jesus' forerunner in his ministry to Israel, in his fateful conflict with earthly authorities, and in his brutal death (6:7–13; 9:13)."[6] Just as John is "handed over" (1:14), Jesus will be "handed over" (3:19; 9:31; 10:33; 14:10, 11, 21, 41, 42, 44; 15:1, 15). Jesus begins his ministry with no illusions about where it is heading.

6. How is it different to read 1:14–45 with that echo of impending death than to read these events without that awareness, the way they appeared to onlookers at the time?

The coming of God's kingdom is one of Mark's central themes. God's reign is not in a geo-political place "but [is] a dynamic event in which God intervenes powerfully in human affairs to achieve his unfading purposes."[7]

GOING DEEPER

No minister of an earthly sovereign would ever announce, "So and so has become king! If it pleases you, accept him as your king!" Such a blasé, noncommittal declaration certainly did not characterize the news of a Roman emperor's ascension to the throne. The very announcement that so and so is king contains an implicit demand for submission. Jesus' announcement that God is king contains the same absolute demand. The divine rule blazed abroad by Jesus, therefore, requires immediate human decision and commitment: repentance, submission to God's reign, and trust that the incredible is taking place.[8]

7. What does submission to God as king involve for you?

To "believe" the good news (1:15) means more than agreeing with it mentally. It means to trust in a way that affects the way we live. Christopher Marshall explains,

Rational belief is essentially involuntary; a person cannot arbitrarily choose to believe on the spot; it is something that happens to him or her in light of the evidence. Trust, however, is voluntary, an act of the will. Or, again, belief can exist without it immediately affecting one's conduct, whereas trust requires certain consequent actions in order to exist.[9]

8. In 1:16–20, what kind of "belief" do you see Jesus asking from these fishermen? How can you tell?

9. Matthew, Luke, and John describe the events that moved these first disciples to start following Jesus. But Mark leaves all that out and just gives us the command, "Follow me," and the response. What impression of Jesus does this give the reader?

GOING DEEPER

[This first act of Jesus' ministry] raises the question: Who is this who can create such immediate obedience? The miracles that Mark records in [1:21–45] prompt a similar question: Who is this who can do these things?... [T]hey reveal that Jesus, the bringer of the kingdom, has unique power as God's Son and can overmaster demons, offer forgiveness of sins, and effect healing of disease. The powerful call of this one can still transform lives today.[10]

10. "Mark emphasizes the power of Jesus' teaching, not its content."[11] How does Mark show the power of Jesus' teaching in 1:21–28, 38–39?

11. What else can we learn about Jesus from 1:21–45?

Over and over Jesus tells people to keep silent about his miracles (1:25, 34, 43–45). Unlike other teachers and miracle workers, he isn't out to acquire fame and the money that goes with it. He doesn't "trust a faith based on spectacles, and he knows that the clamor of the moment will not last. He also knows that God's power is not revealed solely through miracles. It becomes clearest in the crucifixion, but those who want only miracles can see nothing."[12]

12. How does unsought fame get in the way of Jesus' priorities in 1:35–39, 43–45?

How does the love of celebrity affect Christians (and Christian leaders) today?

We have far more information about Jesus than did those fishermen who left their nets and followed him. If we fail to act, we are even more to blame than the crowds in Galilee.

GOING DEEPER

To be a disciple means accepting Jesus' demands unconditionally. Jesus requires absolute obedience and sacrifice. Discipleship in Mark is not part-time volunteer work on one's own terms and convenience. One must be prepared to leave everything to follow him.[13]

13. How do you respond to the idea of leaving everything to follow Jesus? What does (or would) that mean for you?

RESPONDING TO GOD'S WORD

IN YOUR GROUP:

Here is a prayer to begin a time of worship together:

Lord Jesus, you are God's beloved Son. You have defeated evil, and you embrace those who suffer. You have all authority, and you call us to leave things behind in order to follow you. You baptize your followers with the Holy Spirit. Please show us how to follow you. To what are you calling us? Please give us the courage to leave behind whatever we need to leave in order to follow you. In your powerful name we pray, amen.

ON YOUR OWN:

Reflect on the words "Come, follow me." See yourself in the scene in 1:16–18 as one of those whom Jesus calls. What do you see and hear? Picture the lake and the boat. Smell the fish. What do the nets represent that you are leaving behind? What do you feel when Jesus calls you? What do you do? What do you say to him?

NOTES

1. Garland, 88.
2. This section is based on *The NIV Application Commentary: Mark* (hereafter referred to as *NIVAC: Mark*), by David E. Garland (Grand Rapids: Zondervan, 1996), 41–57.
3. Garland, 48.
4. Garland, 52–53.
5. This section is based on *NIVAC: Mark*, 58–91.
6. Garland, 58.
7. Garland, 59.
8. Garland, 60.
9. Marshall, Christopher D. *Faith as a Theme in Mark's Narrative.* Society for New Testament Studies Monograph Series 64 (Cambridge, England: Cambridge University Press, 1989), 56, quoted in Garland, 66.
10. Garland, 79.
11. Garland, 70.
12. Garland, 76–77.
13. Garland, 84.

WHO SPEAKS
FOR GOD?

Mark 2:1–3:6

I magine that a young man who has obvious leadership abilities joins your church. Many in the congregation are impressed with him. But some have concerns. He invites gang members to his house. He says your church's understanding of how to live a godly life is flawed. Not only does he disregard the practices he disagrees with, he publicly flouts them. He even claims the authority to forgive sins. One of your elders complains, "This guy acts like he thinks he's God."

This is what the Pharisees faced. In their society, they were the ones who were most committed to living pure and holy lives. Jesus shared their zeal for the Lord, but more and more he claimed authority beyond the rabbis, beyond even King David—the authority only God has. It was impossible for the Pharisees to imagine that he might be the Messiah, let alone God incarnate. The only other option was that he was a dangerous cult leader who needed to be dealt with in the strongest way.

Jesus' fame was spreading like wildfire, and the opposition to him closed ranks just as fiercely, determined to douse the blaze before it consumed the countryside. We prefer to see ourselves as like Jesus rather than the Pharisees, but are we really?

HEALING AND FORGIVENESS[1]

Read Mark 2:1–12.

Jesus is back in Capernaum after a ministry tour around Galilee. Crowds. Relentless fans. Everything but TV cameras. He's teaching in a house with a roof thatched of reeds, branches, and dried mud when broken stalks and clods of dirt begin falling down from the ceiling.

1. As in 1:25–27, Jesus does something that causes onlookers to question. How is the questioning in 2:6–7 like and unlike the questioning in 1:25–27?

It's one thing to display authority over unclean spirits. But authority to forgive sins? "To presume to forgive sins is an arrogant affront to the majesty of God, which appropriately can be labeled blasphemy."[2] This is not a priest declaring sins forgiven on the basis of repentance, restitution, and sacrifice (see Lev. 4–5; 16; 17:11). This is acting like God. Either the prophecy of Isaiah 33:22, 24 is being fulfilled before their eyes and the kingdom of God has come, or this is blasphemy worthy of death (Lev. 24:16).

2. Jesus forgives the paralyzed man in response to his friends' faith (2:5). But what faith does he ask from the paralyzed man in 2:9–11?

3. Even after they see the paralyzed man walk away, the teachers of the law aren't able to put faith in Jesus as one with authority to heal and forgive. What do you make of that? Do you find their response understandable? Nonsensical? Why?

4. How is Jesus' ability to forgive this man's sins connected to what he's going to do on the cross?

Jesus connects this man's paralysis to his sin. Modern culture is uncomfortable with a connection between sin and sickness. But without blaming the sufferer ("your cancer is your fault"), we more and more acknowledge that body, mind, and spirit aren't in separate sealed compartments. Body and soul are one integrated whole whose parts constantly affect each other.

5. As you experience your own and others' suffering and sin, how is Jesus' presence in your life relevant to these experiences?

EATING WITH SINNERS[3]

Read Mark 2:13–17.

GOING DEEPER

Levi ... is stationed at an intersection of trade routes to collect tolls, tariffs, imposts, and customs, probably for Herod Antipas. Toll collectors were renowned for their dishonesty and extortion. They habitually collected more than they were due, did not always post up the regulations, and made false valuations and accusations (See Luke 3:12–13).[4]

6. What do we learn about Jesus from the fact that he calls a tax collector in the same way as he called the fishermen in 1:16–20?

[Levi's] obedience [to the call] marks an even more radical break with his past. The other disciples can always go back to fishing (John 21:3), but not so a toll collector who abandons his post.[5]

7. In calling and eating with sinners, is Jesus saying their sin doesn't matter? Explain.

The Pharisees were passionate about living holy lives for a holy God. They "represented an attitude that approached sin from the preventive side. They wanted to make and enforce rules that would safeguard people from becoming impure and immoral. Jesus represented an attitude that approached sin from the creative side, seeking to reclaim the impure and immoral."[6]

8. How do Christians today use rules to safeguard people from becoming immoral?

What do you see as the pros and cons of doing that?

What do you think would happen if churches focused instead on reclaiming immoral people?

Christians have often treated some classes of people as irredeemable (unless they prove themselves worthy by cleaning up their lives before they start attending our church). We say we believe that no one has to earn God's love, but a woman dressed like a prostitute and smelling of cigarette smoke is unlikely to be quickly befriended if she shows up at many of our women's Bible studies.

But Jesus neither looks down on such people nor fears they will contaminate his purity. Instead, he "contaminates them with God's grace and power. He is not corrupted by sinners but transmits blessing on them.... He does not regard his holiness as something that needs to be safeguarded but as 'God's numinous transforming power,' which can turn tax collectors into disciples."[7]

9. How do you typically respond to social outcasts (or do you avoid them)?

NEW WINESKINS[8]

Read Mark 2:18–22.

Over and over, people question Jesus. "Why does this fellow talk like that?" (2:7). "Why does he eat with ... sinners?" (2:16). Now the question is why he doesn't encourage his disciples to fast, as other zealous Jews do.

GOING DEEPER Mark's gospel is full of the sound of ripping. The heavens rip open at the baptism (1:10). Caiaphas, the high priest, tears his garment when confronted with Jesus' claim to be the Christ, the Son of the Blessed One (14:63). The temple veil is ripped from top to bottom when Jesus dies on the cross (15:38). The rips signify "the end of the old and the birth of the new."[9]

10. What are we meant to understand about God's kingdom from the imagery of the bridegroom?

From the old wineskins that rip?

TWO SABBATH DEBATES[10]

Read Mark 2:23–3:6.

Things really get nasty when Jesus critiques the Pharisees' interpretation of Bible passages about the Sabbath, because he implies that they've misread the Scriptures completely. Essentially he asks, "Which is more important, rules or people?"[11]

11. How do the Pharisees treat rules as more important than people in 2:23 – 3:6?

Are there any ways in which Christians today put rules ahead of people? Explain.

Even more outrageously, Jesus compares himself to King David (2:25 – 26; see 1 Sam. 21:1 – 6), whose personal authority made it okay for him to disregard a biblical command about sacred bread in the tabernacle. Jesus not only claims David's authority but calls himself "Lord even of the Sabbath" (2:28).

The Pharisees have "stubborn hearts" (3:5). This doesn't mean emotional coldness but thickheadedness. In the Bible, "The heart [is] the place where one [makes] decisions.... It seems that nothing Jesus can say or do will pierce the thick armor of moral insensitivity that encases the Pharisees' minds."[12]

12. What can we do to have less stubborn minds and wills so that Jesus can get through to us?

RESPONDING TO GOD'S WORD

IN YOUR GROUP:

Pray about the place of rules in your lives and the ways you seek holiness:

> *Lord Jesus, we long to live pure and holy lives the way you did when you lived as a man on earth. Contact with sinners didn't corrupt you, because you were so full of the Holy Spirit that holiness overflowed from you to others. You didn't need to protect your purity, because love welled up in you from a pure heart. You were able to tell when rules were useful and when they got in the way of caring for people. Make us people who are so full of the Holy Spirit that holiness overflows from us and we don't need to fear contact with sinners. Show us our blind spots and the stubborn places in our hearts. In your powerful name, amen.*

ON YOUR OWN:

Prayerfully picture yourself in the scene in 2:15–17. You are one of Jesus' disciples, and he has brought you here to eat with sinners. You have never had social contact with people like this before. What do you see and hear? What are the others at the dinner doing and saying? What do you feel as you share this meal and try to engage in conversation with these people? What do you think and feel when you hear what the Pharisees say? When you hear what Jesus says?

NOTES

1. This section is based on *NIVAC: Mark*, 92–100.
2. Garland, 94.
3. This section is based on *NIVAC: Mark*, 101–104, 110–111.
4. Garland, 103.
5. Garland, 104.
6. Garland, 111.
7. Garland, 112.
8. This section is based on *NIVAC: Mark*, 104–124.
9. Garland, 106.
10. This section is based on *NIVAC: Mark*, 106–124.
11. Garland, 116.
12. Garland, 108.

FRUITFUL AND UNFRUITFUL SOIL

Mark 3:7–4:20

In her book *All Is Forgiven: The Secular Message in American Protestantism*, Marsha Witten described a direct-mail ad she received from a new church in her neighborhood. "It trumpeted itself as a 'new church designed to meet your needs,' with 'positive, practical messages which uplift you each week.' The topics were about how to feel good about yourself, how to overcome depression, how to have a full and successful life, how to handle money, how to handle stress, and so on. She noted that it offered a 'cheerful, practical list of the social and psychological pleasures one might receive from affiliation within its church, with no mention whatsoever of faith or God, let alone of suffering or spiritual striving.'"[1]

This church had likely done its homework and learned what its target market wanted. If Jesus had dealt with his target market in this way, he could have lived a long and comfortable life as a superstar preacher. Instead, even in the early months of his ministry the shape of his teaching made conflict unavoidable. He was deliberately sorting his audience into insiders and outsiders—not attractive versus unattractive people, smart versus slow, or big donors versus the less affluent, but rather those willing to put in effort to understand him and those unwilling. His listeners were self-selecting as potentially fruitful disciples or barren fans and enemies.

CROWDS, RELATIVES, AUTHORITIES, AND DISCIPLES[2]

Read Mark 3:7–35.

Here we see how the crowds, the demons, the Jerusalem authorities, Jesus' relatives, and his disciples each respond to him. He appoints the Twelve primarily to "be with him" (3:14) and secondarily to be sent from him. They will be "the witnesses to his ministry, who have learned from him and are qualified to pass on and authenticate the traditions about him (see Luke 1:2)."[3] They will be the new leaders of God's people, as the old leaders show themselves unfit.

1. How does Jesus deal with his disciples differently than he does the crowds in 3:7–12?

   In 3:13–19?

There is a difference between hanging around with Jesus and truly being *with* him. The Twelve must follow wherever he leads, even into hard work for others' benefit, opposition, and the suffering of the cross.

GOING DEEPER

To be with Jesus is therefore far more difficult than it sounds, and we should be careful ... not to soft sell the task of discipleship. The many hymns that exult in being with Jesus, such as "In the Garden," may mislead us into thinking only in terms of the joys we share with him as we tarry in some idyllic setting.... To be with Jesus in [the garden of] Gethsemane (14:33) was certainly no picnic.[4]

2. For Jesus' disciples, what were the hard parts of being with him? (See, for instance, 3:20–22.)

What are the hard parts of truly being with Jesus (as opposed to hanging around with him) today?

Mark structures 3:20–35 like a sandwich: Jesus' family sets out to take charge of him, then he engages with the Jerusalem authorities, and then his family arrives. In this way Mark draws a shocking parallel between Jesus' family, who might think they have his best interests at heart, and the religious leaders who hate him. Both are trying to shut down his ministry—his family because they fear he's crazy, and the authorities because they claim he's demonized.

3. Family was hugely important in Jewish culture. How does Jesus redefine family for his disciples (3:31–35)?

4. What are some examples of doing God's will that Jesus is talking about?

How can Christians today act as family to one another?

5. At this stage of the story, how would each of the following groups answer the questions "Who is Jesus?" and "What is an appropriate response to him?"

The crowds

The demons

The disciples

Jesus' family

The teachers of the law

GOING DEEPER

The unforgivable sin, blasphemy against the Holy Spirit in this context (3:29), is "deliberately scorning the power and forgiveness of God."[5] The teachers of the law deny that the Holy Spirit is at work in Jesus' ministry.

The definition of this sin is what makes it unforgivable. "[R]ejecting Jesus out of ignorance is one thing, but attacking the power by which he works is far more serious. If one is weak, one can be encouraged. If one is ignorant, one can be informed. If one is willfully blind and deaf and rejects help, what can be done? One has cut oneself off from what might lead to repentance."[6] God cannot forgive as long as his grace extended to us in Jesus Christ is attributed to powers of darkness. He did forgive the apostle Paul whose sin before his conversion was similar when he condemned and persecuted God's work in the infant church (Gal. 1:13–14; Phil 3:5–6). This suggests that though the sin is unforgivable as long as the blaspheming behavior persists, one can move from a stance of blasphemy to a stance of belief.

THE PARABLE OF THE SOILS[7]

Read Mark 4:1–20.

In 3:23 Jesus stops giving the teachers of the law direct explanations as if they were honest inquirers and starts dealing with them "in parables." That is, he starts using enigmatic stories that tease the mind into discovering the truth for itself. He does not simply want to rout them in debate but to entice them to think together with him ... if they are willing to open up their minds to God. If they are unwilling, then his story-puzzles give them the freedom to choose ignorance (4:11–12).

6. In the parable of 4:3–8, 15–20, what kind of soil are the teachers of the law? Explain.

Jesus uses the verb "to hear" thirteen times in chapter 4, and hearing is the key idea. "Each type of soil hears the word but reacts differently (4:15, 16, 18, 20)."[8]

7. Jesus' disciples react to the parable by asking a genuine question for understanding (4:10). Jesus rewards this reaction with a straightforward answer. Why is a genuine question a good response to Jesus' teaching?

What are other reactions to Jesus' teaching that are ultimately unfruitful? (Consider the parable of the soils, reactions of people in Mark's gospel, and any other reactions you've observed.)

A parable "is a summons 'to look beneath the surface.' ... Everyone may listen, but not everyone can catch what Jesus says."[9] The key is to care enough about Jesus to pursue him for answers and then do what he says.

In 3:7 – 35 Jesus divides insiders from outsiders — those who commit themselves to be with him and to do God's will and those who misunderstand him and consequently interfere with his work. In 4:1 – 20 his teaching creates a split between those who gather around him to learn the mysteries of the kingdom (4:10, 34) and those who do not.

8. Mark wrote for an audience facing serious trouble or persecution (cf. 4:17) for their faith. Some did fall away because they weren't deeply rooted in Christ. How can we prepare ourselves to face suffering well?

9. How should we deal with "the worries of this life, the deceitfulness of wealth and the desires for other things" (4:19) so that they don't make us unfruitful?

Jesus used parables to separate the insiders from the outsiders, but he excludes nobody from his circle of insiders — people exclude themselves. "Outsiders simply do not regard what he says to be critical enough to bother joining the disciples around Jesus in order to receive illumination."[10] He talks to outsiders in riddles, "So that they may ... indeed hear but not understand; because the last thing they want is to turn and have their sins forgiven."[11]

10. Have you ever been a person who didn't want more information about Jesus? Or, do you know anyone who is like that? Explain.

11. Some Christians act as if the church's job is to keep insiders safe and outsiders out. How do you think Jesus wants disciples to act toward outsiders? Toward insiders?

The sower sows the word of God generously even in unpromising ground. "The word of God will not fail (Isa. 55:10–11), and therefore one should not despair over the apparent failures, the blindness of unfaith, the defections, or the pernicious opposition. One can be assured the harvest will come from the response of the good soil."[12] Some failure is inevitable because "[s]ome will reject the truth no matter how it comes."[13]

12. Jesus has entrusted the sowing of the word to us. What is your role in that?

How do you deal with the inevitability of some failure as you do this task?

RESPONDING TO GOD'S WORD

IN YOUR GROUP:

Give each person a chance to share what they believe God is saying to them through the parable of the soils, perhaps about what kind of soil they are (or are tempted to be), or about their participation in the work of sowing the word in the world. After each person shares, pause to pray for them.

ON YOUR OWN:

Spend some time reflecting on what God might be saying to you through the parable of the soils. If you have questions, as the disciples did, ask him your questions. Ask for discernment as well as for strength and courage to do what he is asking of you. Approach him with an attitude of willingness: "Lord, I am entirely willing to hear what you are saying and to do what you ask me." Write down something concrete about the area you need to address and one or more steps you need to take.

For example, "The desire for material things interferes with my fruitfulness as a disciple. I put so much energy into entertaining and pursuing that desire that I don't have enough left over for the kingdom of God. Lord, please help me to desire the fullness of your kingdom more than I desire these other things. One step I can take in shifting my priorities is to stop spending X dollars on one desire I am in the habit of indulging (coffee, more-than-minimum television service, take-out food, new clothes, etc.) and direct those dollars to the work of God (my church, a ministry to the poor, missions, etc.)." Or, "One step I can take is changing how I spend my time so that I can volunteer time for the work of God."

It's important to be specific about your plan and to follow through. Many of us have structured our expectations by the axiom "more is better" to such a degree that we are simply too cash-strapped to give money away. Downscaling our ideas of "necessities" takes a major reorienting of our minds, but this is one of the Holy Spirit's strongest calls to Christians in our society. This is only one example of a response to the parable, but it is one that resonates with many Christians today.

NOTES

1. Marsha G. Witten, *All Is Forgiven: The Secular Message in American Protestantism* (Princeton: Princeton University Press: 1994), 3–4, quoted in Garland, 170.
2. This section is based on *NIVAC: Mark*, 125–149.
3. Garland, 129.

4. Garland, 138.
5. Garland, 136. This entire "Going Deeper" is summarized from Garland, 135–137.
6. Garland, 136.
7. This section is based on *NIVAC: Mark*, 150–173.
8. Garland, 151.
9. Ibid.
10. Garland, 160.
11. B. Hollenbach, "Lest They Should Turn and Be Forgiven: Irony," *Biblical Translator* 34 (1983): 320, quoted in Garland, 159.
12. Garland, 156–57.
13. Garland, 157.

FEAR AND FAITH

Mark 4:21 – 6:6a

The comic book myth of Superman owes much to the gospel. It concerns an immensely powerful person from another world who lives among us disguised as an ordinary human. When evil strikes, he tears off his disguise, vanquishes the foe, and then returns to a life in which he is often disdained for his ordinariness.

Both the likeness and unlikeness between Superman and Jesus are telling. Jesus is not disguised as a man; he is one, despite his divine origins. To the skeptical onlooker he seems insignificant, a manual laborer, a mere mustard seed of a man. But he has vast powers over natural forces, demonic forces, even disease and death. Like Clark Kent, Jesus avoids publicity and endures scorn. But Clark/Superman requires nothing from those he delivers from evil, while Jesus insists on a response of faith — not just trust when he's wearing his red cape and working wonders, but trust when he seems to be only a carpenter.

FAITH IN THE INSIGNIFICANT[1]

Read Mark 4:21 – 34.

As in 4:1 – 20, Jesus continues to tell parables that can disclose, to those who take the trouble to listen closely, key truths about him and the kingdom he heralds. "The parable of the lamp affirms that God's purpose is not to shroud the light in darkness but to make it manifest to all.... Paradoxically, what is hidden becomes plain by the process of concealing it."[2]

1. In what ways has Jesus been operating like a lamp hidden under a bowl (4:21–22, compare 4:11–12, 33–34)?

What is hidden is meant to be disclosed (4:22). What response from people leads Jesus to disclose more and more of his light (4:23–25)?

What response leaves people in darkness?

As the parables of the lamp and the measure (4:21–25) are a pair, so the parables of the sown seed and the mustard seed are a pair that helps to interpret each other. In both, seeds are sown in or on the ground. "[T]he seed will produce the results inherent within it, although the farmer cannot begin to fathom how the change takes place and though the smallest of seeds looks so unpromising."[3] In both cases, the result of the growth has overtones of the time when history as we know it will end.

2. How is the seed in 4:26–29 deceptively insignificant?

How is the seed in 4:30–32 deceptively insignificant?

How do Jesus and his kingdom seem deceptively insignificant?

3. In what ways do the seeds in these two parables require onlookers to respond with faith? What do onlookers need to trust?

GOING DEEPER [T]he kingdom of God may continue to look like a failure. The tiniest of seeds becomes the greatest of all shrubs, but a shrub is still a shrub, [not something grandiose like a giant redwood.] [T]he kingdom will not fit our expectations or specifications. For those who want ... something more show-stopping and messianic, the kingdom of God as it is manifest in our world will be mostly disappointing. It comes incognito; and up to the very end, one can only trust that Jesus' movement is God's work when all things will finally be revealed.[4]

4. As you listen closely to these parables, what is Jesus saying to you?

Jesus doesn't call us to be successful. He calls us to be faithful, to persevere through discouragement in doing the work of the kingdom, to avoid the allure of grand success, knowing that God will make sure that seemingly insignificant seeds will produce the great harvest.

CALMING THE STORM[5]

Read Mark 4:35 – 41.

A number of boats full of Jesus' followers set off across the several-mile width of the Sea of Galilee. Storms are common there, and fishermen are used to them, but this one is violent enough to scare even seasoned sailors.

5. The disciples interpret Jesus' sleep as a sign of indifference to their plight (4:38). What do you think it's a sign of?

6. Jesus stills the storm with a command. Why are his disciples still terrified after he does this?

Do you think their fear is reasonable? Explain.

The stories in 4:35–5:43 illustrate the predicament we humans find ourselves in: "We live in a fallen world beset by powers of chaos that are out to destroy us"—physical dangers, satanic evil, disease, death. "Our faith is weak, and we do not know in what or in whom we can trust."[6] Jesus' power is the solution to our plight. But will we trust him?

FREEING A DEMONIZED MAN[7]

Read Mark 5:1–20.

Jesus now leads his followers into pagan territory, an unholy land filled with swine and demons and people who care nothing for a deranged man in their midst. He shows that God doesn't just sit waiting for humans to turn to him; he takes the initiative, searching for those who've never searched for him.

As he subdued the forces of nature with words, Jesus now subdues the forces of Satan with words. The demoniac's name, Legion, alludes to the number in a regiment of the Roman army—up to 7,000 men when fully staffed.

7. During the storm, the disciples were desperate to be saved from drowning. What signs of desperation does the demonized man display in 5:2–12?

8. The disciples were afraid after Jesus calmed the storm. The demons are afraid of Jesus when they meet him. And instead of being thrilled to see

the formerly demonized man sitting safe and calm, the people of this region are scared (5:15). Why are they scared?

What does it say about them that instead of welcoming Jesus, they're desperate for him to go away (5:16–17)?

Why don't miracles automatically make people have faith in Jesus?

GOING DEEPER

One newspaper columnist wrote in response to a terrorist bombing that slaughtered many innocent people, including [children and workers in] a day-care center: "From what universe beyond this one that most of us inhabit does this kind of evil arise?" A belief in supernatural evil powers keeps us from whittling down the source of evil to our size and prevents us from deceiving ourselves that we can defeat it alone. People need to recognize that creation is fallen and needs redeeming, for then they will look to the One who has the power to redeem it.[8]

HEALING THE SICK AND THE DEAD[9]

Read Mark 5:21–43.

Here we see Mark's sandwich technique again: He sandwiches the story of the bleeding woman between the two halves of the story of Jairus's daughter so that the two stories interpret each other. Jairus is a rich, respected, high-status male. The woman is inferior because of her gender, has spent all her money, and is a social outcast because bleeding makes a person ritually unclean. "Anyone who has contact with her by lying in her bed, sitting in her chair, or touching her becomes unclean and is required to bathe and to launder clothing."[10] She would disgust most respectable people, the way people today would avoid a street person with tuberculosis.

9. What signs of desperation do you see in Jairus and the woman?

Who in these stories is afraid, and why?

At first the woman treats Jesus as if he were an impersonal source of magical power, according to pagan beliefs of the day. One magic touch will heal. Jesus breaks his custom of secrecy because she needs to know that his healing is personal, a matter of relationship. He calls her to deal with him face to face, and in doing so he treats her as a person worthy of the same attention he gives to the high-status Jairus. Jesus always dignifies those he touches.

10. Jesus expects both Jairus and the woman not just to believe things *about* him, but to take the risk of *acting* in faith. What actions does Jairus have to take by faith, and why are they risks?

What does the woman have to do by faith, and why is it a risk?

GOING DEEPER

Faith is embodied in action. Faith is something that can be seen, like the men digging through a roof to bring their friend to Jesus. It kneels, begs, and reaches out to touch. Belief about Jesus does not bring healing, but faith in Jesus that takes action does.[11]

11. What do these stories—the calming of the storm, the freeing of the demonized man, and the healings of the dead girl and sick woman—reveal about Jesus? What do they say about his identity, mission, character, and priorities?

A PROPHET REJECTED AT HOME[12]

Read Mark 6:1–6a.

After acting as Superman all around the Sea of Galilee, Jesus goes to his hometown, where everybody thinks they know who he is: plain old Clark Kent. Nothing he does can overcome their preformed assumptions about him. They're like people raised in Christian homes who leave the too-familiar faith for something fresh and exotic, thinking, I already know him from the Bible stories of my youth and he hasn't filled my hunger for meaning. They think, "What can he teach me now?"

12. Who are you in the stories of 5:1–6:6a? Are you a panicked disciple, a healed person sent back to spread the word, or someone desperate for healing and trying to trust? Or are you a Gerasene villager afraid to get involved with Jesus' war against evil, or perhaps someone as familiar with and blasé about Jesus as those in his hometown? Explain your answer.

To what risky act of faith is Jesus calling you?

RESPONDING TO GOD'S WORD

IN YOUR GROUP:

Jesus' call in 4:21–34 is to listen closely to him. His call in 5:1–6:6a is to demonstrate faith through action. What action might he be asking from your group? Maybe someone in your group is suffering like the bleeding woman and needs some focused attention, touch, and prayer. If so, gather around that person, touch them, and pray, asking God for healing and freedom.

Or maybe God is asking your group to do something together to serve him. In session 5 you'll see Jesus involving his disciples in his ministry of healing the sick, feeding the hungry, and combating evil. Now is a good time to start asking him how he might want to involve you in his ministry, perhaps in outreach to the homeless or to the addicted or those in prison. Pray about any fears that arise when you're challenged to act on your faith.

> *Lord Jesus, you have power over the world of storms and earthquakes, over the forces of evil, over disease and death. Our natural response is to fear these dangers, to fear trusting you to carry us through them, and to fear your call to join you in your mission of acting on behalf of people who suffer. Sometimes your kingdom seems as hidden and insignificant as a mustard seed, but by your grace we choose to have faith that you will bring fruitfulness when we sow tiny seeds. Please show us how you would like us to serve you, both individually and as a group. We ask this in your mighty name. Amen.*

ON YOUR OWN:

Adapt the preceding prayer for your personal use. As you answered questions 4 and 12, what did you sense God saying to you? Pray back to him what you believe he's saying, tell him about your fears, asking him to empower you to act in faith. If you're not already involved in a ministry to those in need, is this something you might explore?

NOTES

1. This section is based on *NIVAC: Mark*, 174–188.
2. Garland, 175.
3. Garland, 179.
4. Garland, 182–183.
5. This section is based on *NIVAC: Mark*, 189–200.
6. Garland, 198.
7. This section is based on *NIVAC: Mark*, 201–217.
8. Garland, 211.
9. This section is based on *NIVAC: Mark*, 218–229.
10. Garland, 219.
11. Garland, 227.
12. This section is based on *NIVAC: Mark*, 230–238.

THE TRAINING
OF THE TWELVE

Mark 6:6b–56

Hundreds of pilots in Britain's Royal Air Force died in World War II, and chaplains had the challenging job of comforting the families in their grief. One RAF chaplain, Stuart Barton Babbage, gave a sermon about the inner peace Christians could have with regard to death, and one person who heard it disputed his tone. That person was C. S. Lewis. As Babbage later recalled, " 'No,' he said, 'death is dreadful and we are right to fear it ... [It] is not a very little thing and it is horrible.' "[1]

Like a chaplain in wartime, Mark has the challenging job of proclaiming the gospel in a way that takes seriously the threat of death hanging over his readers, but that also testifies to God's power in the midst of mortal danger. Up to this point in Mark's story, the disciples have just been along for the ride, but now it's time for them to start participating in Jesus' ministry, to learn by doing. Jesus and the reader know what the disciples don't, that Jesus is training them to take over after he's gone, and taking over his ministry will mean taking over its risks.

MINISTRY IN DANGEROUS TIMES[2]

Read Mark 6:6b–30.

When Jesus sends out the Twelve with his message of repentance, he gives them the authority that backs up his own message: authority to heal and to drive out unclean spirits. "[W]e might expect him to give detailed advice on what to do when they encounter unclean spirits ... but instead he instructs them on what not to pack for the trip."[3] He also tells them to expect rejection.

1. Did traveling Galilee in weakness, dependence, and poverty fit with a message of repentance better than traveling first-class would have? Explain your view.

GOING DEEPER

The Twelve's mission carries a flavor of urgency: Repent *now* and serve the true King. The messengers do not invite Israel to accept God's reign if it suits them; they confront people with a yes or no decision, so that there can be no middle ground. If they reject the message, they will deprive themselves of the opportunity to receive healing and deliverance. If they continue in their dogged defiance, they will face the judgment of God.[4]

2. What place does such an urgent "yes" or "no" tone have in our communication of the gospel today?

"Jesus sends his disciples out to tackle evil that is larger than personal evil and to deliver people from whatever enslaves them."[5] Whether or not we see ourselves as called to drive out demons, the church is called to stand up and confront evil wherever it manifests: when family members abuse children, when corporations defraud customers, when criminals lure girls into sexual slavery. "The temptation is for us to retreat from the world or to overlook the evil in our midst."[6]

3. What goes on inside you when you think about confronting the world's evils, whether globally or close to home?

What is your role in confronting evil? What is your church's role?

What about your role and your church's role in offering healing?

The disciples' departure on their first mission trip (6:6b–13) and their report afterward (6:30–32) "sandwiches the account of the death of John the Baptizer (6:14–29)."[7] Mark links these events. John's story shows what's on the horizon for anybody who calls the powerful to repentance. John's fate will be Jesus' fate—and the fate of most of the Twelve, and the fate of many of Mark's readers, and perhaps our fate too, if we consistently choose to follow Jesus.

4. Compare 6:14–29 to whatever you know about what will happen to Jesus. What similarities do you see? (You also might look at 14:53–65 and 15:1–15.)

Herod's marriage to his half-brother's ex-wife is doubly incestuous, because she is the daughter of another of his half-brothers. And his response to his step-daughter's sensual dancing (either permitted or prompted by her mother) also hints at incestuous lust. Herod knows no taboos, and his drunken party with its dancing girls is pagan and utterly un-Jewish.

5. When you think about the disciples' ministry of preaching repentance, defeating evil spirits, and healing the suffering (6:12–13) side by side with the account of what happened to John, what thoughts about ministering in the power of the Spirit do you have?

THE MESSIAH'S FEAST[8]

Read Mark 6:31–44.

6. Mark doesn't tell us how successful the Twelve's mission was. Instead, how does he convey the people's hunger for what Jesus offers (6:30–34)?

Jesus' banquet for this rabble foreshadows the feast the Messiah will celebrate (Isa. 25:6–8), the wedding supper of the Lamb (Rev. 19:9), the feast to which God already invites his people (Isa. 55:1–2). Jesus' final Passover feast with his disciples will be another such foretaste (Mark 14:12–26). Jesus' banquet "contrasts with the drunken debauchery of Herod's feast … (6:22). Herod's feast, with its exotic fanfare and dancing girls, cannot ultimately satisfy human hunger. Herod serves up only death…."[9]

7. This story of the feeding echoes many Old Testament stories. Moses, Elijah, and Elisha all miraculously fed people by the power of God. How is feeding the hungry with actual physical bread such a potent statement of what God does?

8. What echoes do you see between this story and Psalm 23?

9. What role do you think feeding the hungry should have in our ministry today?

Like the disciples, we often count our income and our possessions and say we don't have enough to "venture out in faith to help others. When Christians on average give about 3 percent of their income to the church and even less of their time in direct ministry, we know that we do have enough but we are keeping it for ourselves."[10]

THE LORD REVEALED[11]

Read Mark 6:45–56.

Leaving the scene of a miracle they can't wrap their minds around, the disciples find themselves on the lake again, not in a storm but fighting against the wind after hours of strenuous rowing. Jesus sees their distress and goes to them during the darkest part of the night. "Just as Jesus did not first feed the hungry multitudes but taught them (6:34), so he does not first rescue the disciples ... but tries to teach them something by passing by them."[12] In the Old Testament, the verb "to pass by" (6:48) is used for instances when God reveals himself (e.g., Ex. 33:19, 22; 34:6; 1 Kings 19:11).

10. Walking on water has become a cliché, a topic of jokes. But imagine the scene as it was for the disciples. What do you see? Hear? Feel?

What do Job 9:8 and Isaiah 43:16 tell you about what a Jew steeped in the Old Testament should think when he sees this?

Jesus calls out, "It is I" (6:50). In the Greek Old Testament, this phrase *ego eimi* is the same one used to translate God's declaration of his name, "I Am Who I Am" (Ex. 3:14). Jesus is saying, "Don't be afraid. I Am is with you."

11. The idea of God appearing in the flesh was completely alien to Judaism. How do the disciples deal with it?

What is an appropriate response to such an event?

Jesus comes to his disciples in their distress and shows patience when they fail to understand. "There is no rebuke, only calm assurance."[13] He "does not rescue his disciples out of the sea but enables them to continue the voyage."[14]

12. When have you been too dense or too frightened to recognize God's blessing and bounty (as in the miraculous feeding) or his presence and care (as on the lake)?

As you consider both the dangers of following Jesus and his powerful presence in this section of Mark, what is God saying to you?

RESPONDING TO GOD'S WORD

IN YOUR GROUP:

In this section of Mark's gospel, the disciples start sharing the work of Jesus' ministry. How can you, as a group or two by two, share in this work? How can you together proclaim the gospel, feed the hungry, do something practical for the sick, or join in opposing evil? Perhaps some group member other than the leader can be the point person for this service project. What ministry opportunities does your church offer, or what ministries are there in your community? Make a plan.

> *Lord Jesus, you have power over the wind and the waves, over the forces of evil, over disease and death. You care deeply for the hungry, the sick, those afflicted by evil, and even your confused and stubborn disciples. Our natural response is to fear the dangers, to fear trusting you to carry us through them, and to fear your call to join you in your mission of acting on behalf of people who suffer. But you are the great I AM, God in human flesh. You courageously proclaimed the truth despite rejection, and even knowing that a fate like John the Baptist's awaited you. Please fill us with your courage. Help us to grasp the authority and the mission you are giving us. Enable us to overcome the parts inside us that draw back from action. Soften our hearts. We make ourselves available to you, and we ask you to guide us in your powerful name. Amen.*

ON YOUR OWN:

To what area of service is God calling you? How can you overcome obstacles such as busyness and fear? Talk to God about your desires and about the obstacles you face. Adapt the prayer on page 62 for your personal use.

NOTES

1. Carolyn Keefe, ed., *C. S. Lewis: Speaker and Teacher* (London: Hodder & Stoughton, 1971), 92, quoted in Michael Ward, *Planet Narnia: The Seven Heavens in the Imagination of C. S. Lewis* (New York: Oxford University Press, 2008), 300.
2. This section is based on *NIVAC: Mark*, 239–251.
3. Garland, 240.
4. Garland, 242.
5. Garland, 142–143.
6. Garland, 144.
7. Garland, 240.
8. This section is based on *NIVAC: Mark*, 252–260.
9. Garland, 254.
10. Garland, 260.
11. This section is based on *NIVAC: Mark*, 261–269.
12. Garland, 261–262.
13. Garland, 267.
14. Garland, 268.

UNCLEAN?

Mark 7:1 – 8:21

We live in the most sanitary conditions in history. Nineteenth-century scientists discovered that germs were the source of many illnesses—illnesses that had seemed to come from the devil or from bad "humours" in the air. In the twentieth century, Americans went to war against germs and dirt. Sewage systems and waste-water treatment plants freed millions from the risk of waterborne epidemics. By the 1950s, many a housewife's sense of self-esteem came from the spotlessness of her home. By the 1990s, hand soap containing antibacterial agents was in many bathrooms, despite doctors' warnings that overuse of such agents could breed resistant bacteria. Grocery stores provide wipes to sterilize cart handles so that one need not risk acquiring a previous customer's virus. Cleanliness may not be next to godliness, but it does provide a sense of security from invisible enemies.

The debate over clean and unclean between Jesus and those around him had nothing to do with germs. Washing hands and separating from whole classes of people were meant to ensure one's moral purity. Jesus' thoughts on what really infects a person are as unsettling now as they were then.

THE TRADITION OF THE ELDERS[1]

Read Mark 7:1–23.

The religious laws in the books of Exodus and Numbers commanded priests serving in the tabernacle (and later in the temple) to wash their hands and to let their households eat only meat that was ceremonially clean. The Pharisees extended these purity laws to laypeople and to all food so that God's holiness need not be restricted to the temple but would pervade the whole nation. They genuinely wanted to give laypeople precise guidance on what to do to be holy. The desire for holiness was laudable, but Jesus didn't think much of their practices.

1. The Pharisees publicly challenge Jesus about why his disciples don't follow the tradition concerning hand washing. He doesn't answer their question but instead critiques their whole enterprise. What problems does he find with their traditions (7:5–13)?

2. Do you practice any valuable Christian traditions? If so, name one or two.

3. Are there any traditions in your church or your branch of Christianity that sometimes get more attention than yielding one's heart (one's core being) to God? If so, what are they?

4. Are there any traditions in your church that sometimes get in the way of God's command to love our neighbors? If so, what are they?

5. In 7:14–23, Jesus explains to the crowd and then to his disciples in private why he thinks hand washing is irrelevant to their moral purity. Why does he think that?

Jesus does not differ with the Pharisees only over details such as washing hands; he rejects their whole approach to God's law. They are concerned with surface impurity and piety; Jesus is concerned about internal purity that one cannot wash away by washing the hands. They do not understand that true holiness that imitates God and opens one up to God is something internal....The heart is the core of motivation, deliberation, and intention.[2]

6. What implications do Jesus' words in 7:20–23 have for Christian discipleship or spiritual formation?

JESUS AND THE PAGAN WOMAN[3]

Read Mark 7:24–30.

Jesus has just critiqued the boundaries that pious people have set up between themselves and things that supposedly cause spiritual contamination. Now he travels far north to the region of Tyre, which is a mainly Gentile area. The Jews believed that while a Jew could be made unclean by touching something unclean, a Gentile was innately unclean. Moreover, Tyre was rich, and the Gentiles there often ate bread from the grain grown in Galilee, leaving the Jewish Galileans hungry. So when a Gentile from hated Tyre comes begging Jesus for help, will he be as gracious to her as he was to the unclean outcasts within Israel?

7. What is Jesus saying in 7:27?

This insult offends most modern readers. We don't expect such harshness from our Jesus, and we're inclined to explain it away. But while even Jesus' disciples are usually too thickheaded to understand his riddles until he spells them out, this pagan woman does understand him. And she neither retorts in pride nor slinks off in shame. Instead "she becomes the first person in the narrative to engage Jesus in a constructive exchange about his mission."[4] His disciples have seen him feed five thousand people on a few loaves, but this foreigner understands much more about the bread he offers than they do, and she won't be put off.

8. Why do you think this woman is willing to accept the place of a Gentile "dog" begging for the crumbs that fall from the Jews' table (7:28)?

9. From time to time, Jesus calls various people "hypocrites," "an evil generation," "brood of vipers," and "dogs." What would you do if you needed Jesus' help and he talked to you the way he talked to this woman? Why would you respond that way?

MORE BREAD FOR GENTILES[5]

Read Mark 7:31 – 8:21.

Jesus now passes through Sidon and down to the Decapolis — into more Gentile regions. Regardless of what he has just said about his bread being first for Jews, he now continues to disregard the boundary between a clean Jew like himself and the supposedly unclean Gentiles. He heals a man who is deaf and mute (7:31 – 37), thereby attracts a crowd, and then repeats his mass feeding miracle, this time for Gentiles (8:1 – 10).

10. What do you think Jesus' disciples should learn from these episodes?

For the Pharisees, Jesus' miracles aren't enough proof that he speaks for God, especially because he flouts their traditions. So they ask him for an apocalyptic sign in the heavens (8:11) of the sort that signals that God is about to unleash his end-times wrath on his enemies and raise Israel to glory. He rejects this temptation to be the triumphalist Messiah that everybody wants. He takes his disciples back out in a boat and warns them against the leaven of the Pharisees and Herod (8:15). Unlike our modern yeast, the sourdough leaven used in those days could easily become tainted with bacteria and poison the bread, so in the Old Testament it symbolized the infectious power of evil.

11. What are the disciples supposed to understand from Jesus in 8:14–21?

Why don't they get it?

12. What might Mark be saying by showing us a pagan woman who understands Jesus' riddle about bread, and then showing that his disciples don't understand him, even though they've seen repeated miracles with bread?

13. What bread do you need from Jesus? How badly do you need it?

RESPONDING TO GOD'S WORD

IN YOUR GROUP:

What are the needs in your group? Take time to hear from each person who wants to express a need. Then go to Jesus in prayer with the humility of the desperate woman. Are you willing to keep trusting and pursuing Jesus for what each group member needs even if Jesus initially seems to slam the door in your face?

> *Lord Jesus, we are prone to be hard-hearted like the disciples, to fret about what we don't have rather than trusting you to be the source of everything we need. We also are prone to be proud, or too easily humiliated, so it's hard for us to be persistent when you seem not to respond when we pray. We don't like thinking of ourselves in humble terms like "dogs." We come to you now with our needs, as desperate as the mother in this story, knowing that you alone have the power and the compassion to help us. Amen.*

ON YOUR OWN:

Look at Jesus' list of things in the heart that make a person unclean (7:21–23). Consider each in turn and ask yourself, "Is this a problem in my heart?" Choose one to pray about in particular. Confess ways in which you are already aware of it affecting you, and ask God to help you notice this week any times when this sin bubbles up from inside you.

NOTES

1. This section is based on *NIVAC: Mark*, 270–286.
2. Garland, 275, 276.
3. This section is based on *NIVAC: Mark*, 287–297.
4. Garland, 289.
5. This section is based on *NIVAC: Mark*, 298–319.

THE UNEXPECTED MISSION

Mark 8:22–9:29

E ven among North Americans who have lost interest in orga-
nized religion, Jesus remains popular, perhaps because many
find him so adaptable. The Dalai Lama, the spiritual leader of
Tibetan Buddhism, has written favorably about how Jesus' teaching meshes with the Buddha's. If you're a manly man, you can buy
artwork depicting the muscular carpenter-turned-radical, while
for your children you can buy a picture book showing a fine-
boned Jesus smiling at toddlers and lambs. If you want a Savior
to help you feel good about yourself, many churches will happily
give you that Jesus.

At the midpoint of Mark's gospel, Jesus' disciples have been
traveling with him for some time, and they're pretty sure they've
figured out who he is. But a turning point has come, a moment in
which the question shifts from "Who is Jesus?" (the Messiah) to
"Exactly what has the Messiah come to do?" Like us, the disciples
have a picture in their minds of what they want Jesus to be and
do. And like them, we may need to adjust our mental picture to
the truth of his mission and ours.

A STUBBORN CASE OF BLINDNESS[1]

Read Mark 8:22–9:1.

Some people bring a blind man to Jesus (8:22–26), and the case proves stubborn. Jesus' first effort only half heals the man—he can see somewhat, but things are distorted. Patiently, Jesus applies his power again, and this time the man sees clearly.

This incident mirrors what is going on between Jesus and his disciples. They are thickheaded enough to worry about forgetting to bring bread (8:14–16) even though they are with Jesus, who has twice fed thousands of people on a few loaves. They have a stubborn case of blindness, but Jesus is patiently working to uncloud their sight. In 8:27 he leads them way up north near Caesarea Philippi, a pagan area where Herod the Great built a grand marble temple to honor the Roman emperor as a god.[2]

1. In 8:27–29, how does Peter show that his spiritual blindness has begun to heal?

2. In 8:30–32, how does Peter show that his sight is still distorted?

Why do you suppose what Jesus says in 8:31 is so hard for Peter to accept?

GOING DEEPER

It was by no means obvious that Jesus was the Messiah. A few people were healed, many were fed, but Israel was not yet free from pagan domination. In the first century most Jews believed the Messiah would be a royal figure, the offspring of David, whom God would empower to deliver Israel from her foes. This kinglike figure would be as triumphant as David and as wise as Solomon.... Jesus has not yet delivered on any of these hopes, but Peter brims with confidence nonetheless.[3]

3. Jesus calls Peter "Satan" (8:33). What satanic temptation has Peter thrown at Jesus?

After explaining his own mission, Jesus goes on to say that his followers will have to take the same road (8:34–38). First, they must "deny the self and all self-promoting ambitions."[4]

GOING DEEPER

Denying oneself is the opposite of self-affirmation, of putting value on one's being, one's life, one's position before man or God, of claiming rights and privileges peculiar to one's special position in life or even of those normally believed to belong to the human being as such.[5]

4. How has Jesus denied himself for the sake of others?

5. What goes through your mind when you think about denying yourself to do what Jesus gives you to do? (For instance, what draws you toward or away from denying yourself?)

GOING DEEPER

Cross-bearing refers to self-sacrifice, even to the point of giving one's life.... Jesus does not offer his disciples varieties of self-fulfillment, intoxicating spiritual experiences, or intellectual stimulation. He presents them with a cross.... This particular demand separates the disciples from the admirers. Disciples must do more than survey the wondrous cross, glory in the cross of Christ, and love the old rugged cross, as beloved hymns have it. They must become like Jesus in obedience and live the cross.

To take up your cross means ... "subjecting yourself to shame, to the 'howling, hostile mob.'" Disciples stake their lives on their confession that he is the Messiah and follow him on the way to suffering.... We have only found Christ when we are more concerned about others' suffering than our own.[6]

6. We don't deny ourselves in order to shrivel up and disappear. We deny ourselves in order to endure whatever comes with doing the work of Christ in a hostile world. How is God calling you to love, serve, or witness for Christ in a costly way?

7. What are some things people do to try to save their lives (8:35)?

How do those things lead people to lose their lives?

8. Peter's idea of the Christ is laden with selfish, human fantasies.[7] He wants Jesus to defeat his nation's enemies and rule over a prosperous kingdom, with Peter sharing the power and its perks. What are some of the selfish fantasies that can keep a Christian from embracing and living by what Jesus says in 8:34–37?

A GLIMPSE OF GLORY[8]

Read Mark 9:2–13.

Jesus has appalled his disciples by saying that the road he and his followers must take leads down to the depths of suffering before it ascends to glory. They are about to take that road to Jerusalem, but first he takes three of them to a mountaintop, the Bible's traditional place for special revelation, for a glimpse of glory. Elijah and Moses are Old Testament figures expected to appear "at the dawning of the end time and God's ultimate redemption of Israel."[9]

9. How do you think this glimpse of the glorified Jesus can help disciples as they take the long road of self-denial and sacrifice with him?

Based on Malachi 4:5–6, the teachers of the law say that Elijah will come back just before the Messiah comes to launch an earthly kingdom of messianic splendor. Jesus' words in Mark 9:12–13 mean the teachers have things partly wrong: They expect an end-times triumph, but in fact the "Elijah" God has sent is John the Baptist, who has led the way on the road of courageous witness, suffering, and death.

HELP MY UNBELIEF[10]

Read Mark 9:14–29.

Jesus gave his disciples authority over evil spirits (6:7). But having tasted success, they have fallen into their society's belief that power over spirits comes from the exorcist's technique, such as using the right words to tap into divine power. They think they have the gift and can exercise it at will. But they fail publicly.

10. When Jesus says, "This kind can come out only by prayer" (9:29), what do you think he means?

   * You have to pray the right words.
   * You need to pray really hard when you face a demon like this one.
   * You need to be in consistent prayer, depending on God day by day.
   * You need to pray with firm faith that you will succeed.
   * Prayer with fasting is a good technique that often works.
   * Other: _____

When Jesus says, "Everything is possible for him who believes" (9:23), he doesn't mean that faith can accomplish anything. (Working up the psychological state of strongly believing something can sometimes achieve results, but this is a self-reliant technique that has nothing to do with what Jesus is saying.) Jesus means that those who trust *in God* (not in themselves, or in faith, or in whatever) "will set no limits to the power of God."[11] Faith itself isn't powerful; God is powerful. God-focused faith opens us to God's unlimited power.

11. What can we learn about faith from what Jesus and the boy's father say to each other in 9:23–24?

12. It's not hard to have faith, intellectually, that Jesus is the Christ. It is hard to have the faith in him that moves us to deny ourselves, take the road to the cross, and lose our lives. What in your life or in Jesus' call moves you to say, "I do believe; help me overcome my unbelief"?

RESPONDING TO GOD'S WORD

IN YOUR GROUP:

Pray about the way of the cross and about the ways in which you're sometimes torn between exercising faith and not.

> *Lord Jesus, denying our selfish desires isn't just hard—it's impossible without your help. We believe you are the Christ; please help us overcome the whispers of unbelief that keep us from courageously taking risks in your service. We don't seek suffering, but we want to be willing to accept it when necessary. Please help us. Amen.*

You've talked in previous sessions about serving God together. How is that going? Do you need to take another step?

ON YOUR OWN:

Write a letter to Jesus, telling him about the ambitions and fantasies that hinder you from following him on the way of the cross. Ask him to help you set them aside for his sake. Ask him to show you what your next step is in following him. Thank him for being with you on this road.

NOTES

1. This section is based on *NIVAC: Mark*, 312–313, 320–340.
2. Garland, 323.
3. Garland, 323–324.
4. Garland, 327.
5. Ernest Best, *Following Jesus*, Journal for the Study of the New Testament Supplement 4 (Sheffield, England: JSOT, 1981), 37, quoted in Garland, 333.
6. Garland, 334–335.
7. Garland, 325.
8. This section is based on *NIVAC: Mark*, 341–352.
9. Garland, 344.
10. This section is based on *NIVAC: Mark*, 353–364.
11. A. E. J. Rawlinson, *St. Mark*, Westminster Commentaries (London: Methuen & Co., 1931), 124, quoted in Garland, 355.

THE RIGHT QUESTION

Mark 9:30–10:52

Many folktales tell of a main character (such as Aladdin) who encounters a magical figure (such as a genie in a lamp) who will grant three wishes or answer three questions. Complications often arise when the Aladdin character is less than wise in choosing his wishes or questions.

The people around Jesus are remarkable for asking the wrong questions and requesting foolish things. His disciples argue about, but don't dare ask him directly, "Which of us is the greatest?" The Pharisees want to know, "Is it lawful for a man to divorce his wife?" And a rich man asks, "What must I do to inherit eternal life?" Jesus responds wisely to these people, but the most important question is the one that Jesus himself asks.

WHO IS THE GREATEST?[1]

Read Mark 9:30–50.

Jesus and his disciples are now traveling south through Galilee, heading ultimately toward Jerusalem. On the way he again predicts his betrayal, death, and resurrection. His disciples tune out this message and begin to argue with one another.

1. What is the key to achieving greatness in God's kingdom (9:33–35)?

GOING DEEPER

Ancient culture had no romanticized notions about children. They were not regarded as especially obedient, trusting, simple, innocent, pure, unself-conscious, or humble. Welcoming a child meant welcoming someone considered insignificant. The child had no power, no status, and few rights. A child was dependent, vulnerable, entirely subject to the authority of the father.[2]

2. How would you restate 9:37 in your own words?

3. What involvement do you have with people who are powerless, vulnerable, easily ignored, or low in social status?

Jesus' words in 9:39–41 remind us that good can come from circles outside ours. Still, Jesus is not saying that all God requires for salvation is that others show no hostility to Jesus and his followers. In Mark's world, Jesus' followers were hated and could barely hope to receive a cup of water from outsiders. Today, in countries where Christians are openly persecuted, they can be grateful even when their neighbors are neutral. But neutrality is not enough for salvation.

4. In 9:42–48, Jesus doesn't mean for us to literally cut off hands or feet, but obedience to his point might nevertheless take some radical action. What are some things in our lives that we might need to cut off because they would lead us into sin?

CAN WE DIVORCE?[3]

Read Mark 10:1–16.

The question about divorce comes as a test from people whose approach to God's law is "What can I get away with?" This is not a plea for pastoral advice from someone in a troubled marriage; rather it is the search for a loophole by those who think about marriage wrongly. "The Pharisees need to discover what God commands, not what Moses has permitted."[4] The law of Moses simply imposed rules on divorce to minimize the worst of the damage.

5. What do we have to understand about marriage (10:6–7) in order to understand how God views divorce?

6. Jesus gives his stringent standard on marriage in the context of other stringent standards for discipleship. How would obeying what he says in 9:33–37 affect a person's conduct in a marriage and family?

GOING DEEPER

On the one hand, one must be careful to proclaim God's intention for marriage to be a permanent covenant relationship.... Jesus made radical demands of his disciples and believed that God was working in the world so that they could live up to those demands....

On the other hand, one must also be sensitive not to beat people over the head with the Bible when they are already bruised and broken.... While God hates divorce, the church must always be mindful that God does not hate the divorced person.... It is perhaps more important to ask what the church should be doing to strengthen marriages and prevent divorce than to ask what we should do after a divorce.[5]

7. What do you think Jesus would say to a person who has fallen short of his high standards for denying oneself and acting as a servant, and whose spouse has also fallen short, so that they are now contemplating either divorce or staying together in a loveless marriage?

What do you think Jesus would say to a person who has fallen short, has been through a divorce, and who now wants to live as a disciple?

WHAT MUST I DO?[6]

Read Mark 10:17–31.

Jesus' next questioner approaches him with the flattering words his culture expects. He speaks as "one good man to another" who "assumes that one can find goodness in human resources and accomplishments."[7] Like Paul before his conversion (Phil. 3:6), this man has been blameless in keeping the commandments, and if being a basically good person were enough for eternal life, he would be fine.

8. Jesus loves this man. List the things he tells the man to do in 10:21.

Why do you think it's necessary for this man to sell all his possessions?

9. What do these instructions tell us about what is necessary if one wants eternal life?

Jesus has a lot to say about money in the gospels, and it's consistently negative. He treats wealth not as neutral but as "toxic to the soul."[8] Money incites craving, reverence, and envy. It lures us to trust it rather than God for our security. A habit of self-gratification deadens our willingness for self-sacrifice. Yet Christians who take Jesus seriously about divorce often dance around his warnings about possessions. We like to think we're not the rich he's talking about, but by the standards of his culture and most cultures in the world, any middle-class American is rich.

10. Does sustaining your lifestyle get in the way of your following Jesus? If so, how?

11. It's not just difficult for a rich man to enter the kingdom, it's impossible—just as it's impossible for a camel to pass through a needle's eye (10:25–27). Where do Jesus' words leave us?

WHAT DO YOU WANT ME TO DO FOR YOU?[9]

Read Mark 10:32–45.

As they head toward Jerusalem, Jesus for the third time predicts exactly what is going to happen. Yet James and John still seem to think that whatever suffering lies ahead will be temporary and that soon Jesus will set up a kingdom that runs by the same old rules of power. They can't imagine that the places of honor at his right and left will be taken by two thieves crucified with him (15:27). "Jesus labels the desire to dominate others as pagan."[10]

12. Jesus himself is our model (10:45). Why, then, do you suppose we find it so hard to live by his words in 10:42–44?

RESPONDING TO GOD'S WORD

IN YOUR GROUP:

Jesus asks his friends, "What do you want me to do for you?" (10:36). They bring him the deepest desire of their hearts: they want power and glory. Then in 10:51 he asks a blind beggar the same question. The desire of this man's heart is to see.

Take a moment of silence so that everyone can ponder Jesus' question, "What do you want me to do for you?" Imagine that Jesus is asking you this question (because he is). Then give each person a chance to share their response. Afterward, pray about these desires.

> *Lord Jesus, you want us to desire to see. You want us to desire to see you as you truly are, to see ourselves as we truly are, and the world as it truly is. You want us to desire to follow you so much that we are willing to pay the price. And yet we have other desires too, and we don't know where they fit with what you want for us. We know it doesn't get us anywhere to hide these desires and pretend that we don't want anything other than you if that's not true. We know that some of these are desires you have put into our hearts for good purposes. So we bring our desires to you, and we ask you to show us what to do with them. amen.*

ON YOUR OWN:

When weather permits, go for a walk. Think about how the things you see help you to discern the desires of your heart. Offer these up to the Lord in prayer.

NOTES

1. This section is based on *NIVAC: Mark*, 365–376.
2. Garland, 367.
3. This section is based on *NIVAC: Mark*, 377–393.
4. Garland, 380.
5. Garland, 388.
6. This section is based on *NIVAC: Mark*, 394–408.
7. Garland, 395.

8. Garland, 398.
9. This section is based on *NIVAC: Mark*, 409–418.
10. Garland, 412.

THE FRUITLESS TREE

Mark 11:1–12:27

I t's easy to confuse a busy church with a fruitful one. In a busy church, the staff and key volunteers work long hours providing a cafeteria of programs for all age groups. Core church members may attend events at the church several times a week. Weekend services are exciting and well attended. All this activity may—or may not—be associated with a body of church members who, year by year, are growing more intimate with God, more responsive to the guidance of the Holy Spirit, more loving toward one another and toward outsiders, more able to resist their habitual sins, more generous and compassionate toward the needy, more bold in proclaiming the gospel to the lost. This latter set of qualities is what the New Testament describes as fruitfulness, which is the real measure of a church's success.

In Jesus' day, the temple in Jerusalem was perpetually busy—with priests offering the sacrifices prescribed in the Bible; with staff cleaning up the mess of animal sacrifice; with merchants selling sacrificial-quality animals to worshipers; with money changers who could change foreign money into the temple currency required for tithes and offerings; with teachers, students, and spectators. It was busy, but was it fruitful? When Jesus arrived in Jerusalem, he made his own judgment on that question clear.

THE LORD COMES TO HIS TEMPLE[1]

Read Mark 11:1–11.

Jesus has walked everywhere throughout his ministry, but now he commandeers a colt to ride. An animal never before ridden is suitable for a sacred purpose and worthy of a king. The pilgrims streaming toward the city for Passover strew his path with their garments and palm branches and chant acclamations from Psalm 118:25–26 that mark him as the royal Son of David.

1. Until now, Jesus has avoided calling attention to himself. He has told people to keep quiet about his miracles and his messianic identity. Why do you think he now shifts and makes such a dramatic entry into the city?

2. The shouting crowds think Jesus' entrance into Jerusalem is heading toward a triumphal announcement that he is the Messiah and is about to set up a glorious earthly kingdom. Instead, in 11:1–11 Mark shows Jesus fulfilling Malachi 3:1–2. Read that passage and describe what you think is going on in Mark 11:1.

THE LORD JUDGES THE TEMPLE[2]

Read Mark 11:12–33.

The fig tree incident (11:12–14, 20–25) sandwiches the temple incident in order to explain it. Jesus is making a symbolic, prophetic gesture. The fig tree symbolizes the whole sacrificial and legal system of temple Judaism. Because it is barren, Jesus pronounces judgment on it. "Season" in 11:13 "is not the botanical term for the growing season but the religious term," *kairos*, that denotes the time of God's kingdom in 1:14–15.[3]

3. Jesus is often said to be "cleansing" the temple in 11:15–19, ridding it of abuses. This view may imply that he means to reform it. An alternate view is that he is acting out God's rejection of the temple system. Read this incident closely, and think about it in light of Jesus' coming death and resurrection. Do you think he means to reform or to reject the temple? Why?

Jesus says the Jewish leaders have turned the temple into a "den of robbers" (11:17). "The den is the place where robbers retreat after having committed their crimes."[4] The leaders sin flagrantly (12:38–40) and then retreat to the temple to offer the sacrifices God prescribed to atone for sin. But God's offer of forgiveness through shed blood was never meant to enable people to sin without consequences.

4. Does Jesus' sacrifice on the cross give us license to sin all we want without consequences? Explain your thoughts.

5. In 11:22–26 is Jesus saying that faith in ourselves or in our dreams can be effective if we believe strongly enough? Explain what you think he's saying.

6. Why do you suppose we need to forgive others in order to receive forgiveness (11:25)?

THE VINEYARD OWNER JUDGES HIS TENANTS[5]

Read Mark 12:1–12.

The Jewish leaders are furious at Jesus for attacking the temple — the center of their religion and power (11:18). They challenge him, but he outwits them (11:27–33). He then tells a parable that recalls Isaiah's song about Israel as God's vineyard (Isa. 5:1–7). His parable is targeted not at all Jews, but specifically against these leaders.

7. What is Jesus saying in 12:1–9?

What does it say about the Jewish leaders that they hear this and still go forward with killing Jesus?

In 12:10 Jesus quotes Psalm 118, the same psalm the crowds chanted when he entered Jerusalem. He speaks of a stone and builders, but what are the builders building? Jesus has been talking about the temple, and he'll say more about it in Mark 13. If the parable of the tenants was originally told in Hebrew, Jesus used a wordplay to allude to his destiny on the cross as a result of his rejection in Jerusalem—note the similarity between the murdered "son" (*ben*) of the parable and the rejected "stone" (*eben*)—though this idea is lost in both Greek and English translations. The murdered son becomes the cornerstone of a new building project.

8.   What is the new temple, according to 1 Peter 2:2–5 and Ephesians 2:19–22?

How should this affect the way we live our lives?

GOD AND CAESAR[6]

Read Mark 12:13–17.

GOING DEEPER

The Jewish people lived under a crushing tax burden. They maintained the priests and sacrifices in the temple, as well as paid taxes to the Romans. When the Romans levied an additional tax in AD 6, Judas of Galilee led a revolt, arguing that this new head tax "placed God's own land at the service of foreigners."[7] Roman soldiers brutally crushed the revolt. Jesus and his followers came under similar suspicion as political dissenters.

The head tax was paid with a silver denarius. It showed the emperor's head on one side and an inscription on the other that called him the son of "Divine Augustus." Such images on coins declaring the emperor as the son of a god were, "in effect, a portable idol promulgating pagan ideology."[8] By producing the coin, Jesus' enemies show they have no qualms about carrying the idol into God's temple, where the conversation in Mark 12:13–17 takes place.

9. Caesar's money bears Caesar's image. Where is God's image to be found? (See Gen. 1:26–27.)

What does this say about what it means to give "to God what is God's" (Mark 12:17)?

Caesar and God are not two counterparts, each lord of his own sphere (secular versus sacred). God is Caesar's Lord, "for there is only one Lord of the world, not two."[9] God is Lord of all aspects of life we might call secular, including the workplace, the family, and the government. "We may owe Caesar [or our own government] money, but we do not owe Caesar the love that is directed only to God."[10]

10. What are some ways in which our commitment to God might come into conflict with what our government's laws and leaders say?

THE AFTERLIFE[11]

Read Mark 12:18–27.

The Sadducees were a pro-priestly, aristocratic party within Judaism. They rejected the Pharisees' traditions as well as any beliefs they thought came from something other than the five books of Moses. That included the belief that the righteous would ultimately rise from the dead. They baited Jesus with a question based on the law in Deuteronomy 25:5–10 that said that if a man died with no heirs, his brother should marry his widow and provide an heir.

11. What are popular ideas today of what happens after death?

Jesus says resurrected people "will be like the angels in heaven" (12:25) and therefore not married, yet the word *resurrection* means having a body of some kind, not being a disembodied soul. It is also different from *reincarnation*, which means coming back to this earth with a new body. Our resurrection life is beyond our imagination, and Jesus doesn't try to explain what it will be like.

12. What difference does our hope of resurrection make to our lives now?

RESPONDING TO GOD'S WORD

IN YOUR GROUP:

It's appropriate to greet the Messiah with joy, but bittersweet as we remember that the triumph the crowds hope for is not the one Jesus will bring. Even his disciples will flee when their hopes for an easy-life gospel are dashed. Sing or read Henry Milman's hymn,[12] and then pray to be saved from the fickleness of those who first hailed Jesus with Hosannas.

Ride on, ride on, in majesty!
Hark! all the tribes Hosanna cry;
O Savior meek, pursue Thy road
With palms and scattered garments strowed.

Ride on, ride on, in majesty!
In lowly pomp ride on to die!
O Christ! Thy triumph now begin
Over captive death and conquered sin.

Ride on, ride on, in majesty!
In lowly pomp ride on to die;
Bow Thy meek head to mortal pain,
Then take, O God, Thy power, and reign.

Holy Lord, like Jesus' disciples we cling to the desire for you to fill our lives with triumph and spare us from the crucifixion. But without the cross there will be no triumph. Save us from fickleness, from singing praise songs when things are good but abandoning you when things get hard. Save us from foolish expectations of glory in this life. You—not we, not Caesar—are Lord. We want to give all of ourselves to you and to follow wherever you lead. In the powerful name of Jesus, amen.

ON YOUR OWN:

Set on a table some symbols of your material possessions. You might spread out some paper money, your checkbook, your credit cards. Looking at these things, roll over in your mind Jesus' words: "Give to Caesar what is Caesar's and to God what is God's." What is Caesar's? What is God's? What of yourself do you need to give to God at this point in your life?

NOTES

1. This section is based on *NIVAC: Mark*, 426–431.
2. This section is based on *NIVAC: Mark*, 432–449.
3. Garland, 440.
4. Garland, 439.
5. This section is based on *NIVAC: Mark*, 450–460.
6. This section is based on *NIVAC: Mark*, 461–467.
7. Garland, 462. This entire "Going Deeper" is summarized from Garland, 461–463.
8. Garland, 462.
9. Garland, 463.
10. Garland, 466.
11. This section is based on *NIVAC: Mark*, 468–474.
12. Henry H. Milman, "Ride On, Ride On in Majesty," 1820, nethymnal.org, accessed April 2, 2009.

WHAT MATTERS NOW

Mark 12:28–13:37

A quick Internet search reveals dozens of articles arguing that God is about to start the final cataclysm of earth's history. Many of these articles point to events of the twentieth and twenty-first centuries that suggest we are nearing the crucial moment when history will end. One time line lists major earthquakes from 1950 onward, major wars since World War I, and category 5 hurricanes since 1900. The founding of the nation of Israel in 1948 also figures on many time lines.

Interest in the end times has been high for about two centuries. In 1833 William Miller announced his belief that Christ would return in 1843.[1] He attracted followers nationwide, and the failure of his prediction became known as the Great Disappointment.

Because the Bible clearly says that Jesus is coming back, we have at least two questions to ask on the subject. First, is it possible to predict even roughly when he will come? And second, what should we do in the meantime? Jesus addressed both of these questions in the last few days before his crucifixion.

LOVE THE LORD[2]

Read Mark 12:28–44.

Jesus is still teaching in the temple and facing challenges from various groups of leaders.

1. In 12:29–31, Jesus tells what is most important for us to do while we await his return. Give some examples of what it means to love God with . . .

   All your desires

   All your inner motivation and power

   All your ability to see, think, and form opinions

   All your physical capacity

   All your possessions

GOING DEEPER

[The heart (12:30)] is the center of our inner being, which controls our feelings, emotions, desires, and passions. The heart is where religious commitment takes root.[3] [The soul is our] motivating power that brings strength of will. Together with the heart, the soul determines conduct.[4] [The mind] is the faculty of perception and reflection that directs our opinions and judgments.[5] [Strength refers to] one's physical capacities, including ... possessions.[6]

2. What is one aspect of loving your neighbor that is hard for you?

The expert in the law endorses Jesus' view that love for God and neighbor are more important than temple sacrifices (12:32–33). But in doing so, he assumes a superior position from which he passes judgment on Jesus' teaching. So Jesus says he is not far from God's kingdom — but not in the kingdom either. "To be 'in the kingdom' one must do more than simply approve of Jesus' teaching; one must submit entirely to his authority and person."[7]

3. Many great men — including Mahatma Gandhi and the Dalai Lama — have approved of Jesus' teaching, and even practiced it, without submitting to his authority. Why isn't agreeing with his teaching enough?

4. Is it possible to submit to Jesus' authority without practicing his teaching about love? Explain your view.

The crowd listens to Jesus with delight (12:37). He is clever, and they think he wields the political and military power of King David. They have no idea that in alluding to a regime greater than David's, he subverts their hopes. Herod enjoyed listening to John the Baptist too (6:20), but then killed him.

5. What sins of the teachers does Jesus denounce in 12:38–40?

What does this sort of thing look like when Christians do it?

6. Why is the poor widow in 12:41–44 worthy of praise?

The poor widow intends to give all she has to God, but in fact her money goes to the high priests who control the temple and live in luxury. These same priests will bribe Judas to betray Jesus to them. Likewise, today there are leaders and churches who convince vulnerable people to give them money in God's name but who are not worthy. Jesus gives us clues for discerning leaders who deserve our support, and he also sets us an example of concern for the poor.

BE ALERT[8]

Read Mark 13:1–37.

Jesus now leaves the temple, never to return. His disciples are so impressed with it, and indeed it's a marvel of carved and gilded stone atop Mount Zion. But within forty years, at around the time Mark writes his gospel, the Jews will revolt against Rome; the Romans will besiege Jerusalem; there will be a terrible slaughter; and the Romans will, against all expectation, reduce the temple to rubble.

7. What do you think the disciples thought and felt when Jesus predicted the temple's destruction (13:1–4)?

8. List the events that Jesus predicts in 13:5–13.

List what Jesus tells his disciples to do in these verses, in light of these predictions.

Jesus doesn't give his disciples what they want—a firm timetable with signs (13:4). He gives them what they need—enough information so that they won't be "disheartened by persecution, panicked by wars, fooled by appearances, or led to apostasy by false prophets."[9] What he calls "the beginning of birth pains" (13:8) covers "the entirety of the period during which Jesus' disciples bear witness, suffer persecution, and stand in danger of deception, however long or short that period may turn out to be."[10]

9. Which of these two interpretations of Jesus' words do you think is more accurate, and why?

- An increase in wars, earthquakes, and famines are signs that the rapture and other end-times events are about to happen.
- Wars, earthquakes, and famines will happen, but don't be distracted or discouraged by them, because the important thing is to stay alert and keep proclaiming the gospel.

In 13:14–23, Jesus speaks not about the ultimate end time, but about the war in Judea of AD 66–70 that will lead to slaughter in Jerusalem and the temple's destruction. If he were talking about the end time, fleeing Judea (13:14) would be irrelevant to most believers around the world, and why would anyone care about his possessions (13:15) or the winter (13:18) at the end of the world? Rather, Jesus is concerned for people of his day who need to escape the savagery of the advancing Roman army. The cue to flee Jerusalem comes when they see "the abomination that causes desolation" (13:14). This is probably something done by the Jewish rebels or by the Romans to defile the sacred precincts of the temple, as similar language was used to describe the desecration of the temple by previous armies (e.g., 1 Maccabees 6:7). Mark sees this event as a fulfillment of Daniel's prophecy (Dan. 11:31).

10. In 13:14–20, Jesus doesn't lament the temple's desecration, but he does lament the people's suffering. What does this tell you about him?

In 13:24–27 Jesus talks about his Second Coming. But he neither affirms nor denies that there will be a time gap between the temple's destruction and his return. He "wants to prevent his disciples from trying to nail down a specific chronology of end-time events. . . . He expects his disciples to be ready for anything anytime."[11] He repeats:

- "You must be on your guard." (13:9)
- "So be on your guard." (13:23)
- "Be on guard! Be alert!" (13:33)
- "Keep watch because you do not know when. . . ." (13:35)
- "Watch!" (13:37)

11. What does being on guard involve for you?

12. If "no one knows" when Jesus will return, not even Jesus (13:32), why do you think predicting end-times events is so popular today?

Should we concern ourselves with such predictions? Why or why not?

RESPONDING TO GOD'S WORD

IN YOUR GROUP:

Put your heads together as a group and try to list those news events that have happened during your lifetimes that some have claimed would trigger the final war and last years of history. When those events came and went, discuss what, if any, harmful effects those predictions had.

Pray for God to help you do the things Jesus says in Mark 13:

> *Our gracious and loving Lord, it seems like our news is full of wars, earthquakes, famines, and other natural and man-made disasters. These things trouble us, and we often don't know how to respond. We also hear of cult leaders and other false prophets, and they too harm people. Please protect us and our loved ones from deception, and help us not to be fearful when we hear these bad news events. Show us how we can love you and our neighbors amid disasters and crises. Show us how we can be part of preaching the gospel to all nations. Give us the courage to speak about who you are even when people ridicule us. Deliver us from spiritual laziness so that we can continue to keep watch. In the strong name of Jesus Christ, amen.*

ON YOUR OWN:

Watch this week for opportunities to love your neighbors. One idea is to keep in your car things other than money that you can give to homeless people when you see them. You might give a sack containing a gift card for a fast food restaurant, a bag of nuts, a toothbrush, and a small tube of toothpaste. Homeless people often regret the lack of toiletries as much as food, and in this way you can show care without financing someone's possible addiction.

NOTES

1. *Evidence from Scripture and History of the Second Coming of Christ about the Year 1843,* s.v. Miller, William in *Encyclopaedia Britannica*, 11th ed. (1911) 18:465 accessed online on July 14, 2009 at *http://books.google.com/books?id=4FEEAAAAYAAJ&pg=PA465&dq=william+miller+1833&client=safari.*
2. This section is based on *NIVAC: Mark*, 475–486.
3. Garland, 483–484.
4. Garland, 484.
5. Ibid.
6. Garland, 485.
7. Garland, 477.
8. This section is based on *NIVAC: Mark*, 487–512.
9. Garland, 491.
10. Robert Gundry, *Mark: A Commentary on His Apology for the Cross* (Grand Rapids: Eerdmans, 1993), 739, quoted in Garland, 493.
11. Garland, 500.

BETRAYAL

Mark 14:1–72

From 1963 to 1966, the FBI tapped Martin Luther King Jr.'s phone conversations. Two informants gave the FBI reason to believe that "one of King's closest advisers was a top-level member of the American Communist Party, and that King had repeatedly misled Administration officials about his ongoing close ties with the man."[1] However, even after wiretaps proved that the adviser was no longer involved with the Party and that King had no Communist sympathies, "the FBI continued to distribute utterly misleading reports that declared just the opposite; as one newly released CIA summary from just a few weeks before King's death asserts, 'According to the FBI, Dr. King is regarded in Communist circles as "a genuine Marxist-Leninist who is following the Marxist-Leninist line." ' "[2] FBI chief J. Edgar Hoover insisted King was dangerous and had him under surveillance even on the night of his death. Public figures tread on precarious ground.

The chief priests thought Jesus was dangerous too, and they went from surveillance and false accusations to plotting his death.

THE ANOINTED ONE[3]

Read Mark 14:1–11.

Passover celebrated Israel's liberation from Egypt. Jerusalem's population doubled or tripled as pilgrims flocked to the place where they could buy a lamb and have it sacrificed for the feast. Some believed the Messiah would appear on Passover night to liberate the nation from its current oppression. The temple police were on high alert, as the chance of a riot breaking out was great.

1. *Messiah* means "anointed." Normally a priest or prophet anointed a king, pouring oil on his head. How does Jesus' anointing in Bethany ironically contrast with those expectations (14:3–9)?

2. How do the actions of the woman in 14:3–9 contrast with those of the leaders and Judas in 14:1–2, 10–11?

The blood that Jesus will soon pour out is so priceless that pouring out this costly perfume is fitting. Yet in 14:7 Jesus is not saying that caring for the poor is unimportant. The Lord says in Deuteronomy 15:4–5, 11 that poverty in ancient Israel would be eliminated if God's people would obey him. God calls us both to adore Christ lavishly and to care for the poor sacrificially.

THE LAST SUPPER[4]

Read Mark 14:12–31.

3. Throughout this passage, how does Jesus show that he knows what is going to happen?

What do you think we're meant to conclude about him from his foreknowledge?

4. What emotions are the disciples feeling during this meal (14:17–31)? Why?

5. Compare Mark 6:41; 8:6; and 14:22. What are the similarities in what Jesus does?

What might be the significance of these parallels?

When Jesus breaks the bread and distributes it to the disciples, it means that what has happened to this bread will happen to him. The broken bread given to the disciples also symbolizes that his Passion will benefit them and is an acted-out parable of his offering up his life for the many.[5]

Jesus has fed Jews and Gentiles miraculously, but his disciples have consistently failed to understand that there will always be enough bread because Jesus himself is the bread broken and given.

6. What do Jesus' words and actions regarding the bread and the cup mean for us?

PRAYING OR SLEEPING[6]

Read Mark 14:32–52.

"Deeply distressed and troubled" (14:33) translates a Greek word that suggests "the greatest possible degree of horror and suffering."[7] And in 14:36, "Jesus does not enter his suffering stoically but biblically, with loud lament" like the laments we read in the Psalms.[8] In this moment of waiting for the worst, he pours out his horror and longing without restraint, exploring the limits of his Abba's will without trying to counter it.

7. What can we learn about Jesus from the way he prays in 14:32–36?

How is your way of praying similar or different?

8. In Mark 13, Jesus urged his disciples over and over to keep watch so as to be prepared for the moment of crisis. He warned them not to be found sleeping (cf. 13:36). Yet here they fall asleep even though he warns them to watch and pray even as he is praying. How does their failure to watch and pray in 14:32–42 affect what happens in 14:43–52?

GOING DEEPER

Waiting can be the most intense and poignant of all human experiences— the experiences which, above all others, strip us of affectation and self-deception and reveal to us the reality of our needs, our values and ourselves.... One waits at such moments in an agonizing tension between hope and dread, stretched and almost torn apart between two dramatically different anticipations. A wise person will then steel and prepare himself for the worst; but the very tension in which he waits shows that hope is still present ... in the urgent and secret prayer, "O God, let it be all right." In such hope and prayer there is no weakness, no failure of nerve: torn between rational hope and rational dread one may properly pray for the best while still prepared for the worst.[9]

TRIAL[10]

Read Mark 14:53–72.

9. How does Peter's failure to stay awake and pray affect what happens in 14:53–72?

10. Jesus prays with unrestrained honesty about the horror he feels because of what is coming, and asks his Abba for an alternative. Do you think his prayer makes any difference to what happens in his arrest and trial (14:43–72)? Explain.

In 14:62, Jesus claims to be more than the Messiah. In the messianic tradition, God invites Israel's king to sit at his right hand to symbolize that on earth the king shares God's power (2 Chron. 9:8). But nothing in the Old Testament or in Jewish tradition "explicitly conferred on the Messiah full equality with God on a heavenly plane."[11] Jesus claims that "the Christ is something more than simply the Son of David, an earthly ruler. Jesus extends that image here with the allusion to Daniel 7:13, 'coming with the clouds of heaven.'" He implies that he has divine authority, in heaven and not just on earth. This is either true or blasphemous.[12]

11. Why should the council have believed Jesus' shocking statement? What evidence has there been in Mark's gospel that this is truth and not blasphemy?

Jesus has renamed his disciple Simon as "Peter," a rock. Yet in the high priest's courtyard he shows himself more like the shallow rocky ground in the parable of the sower (4:16–17), the kind of person who receives the word of the kingdom with joy but who falls away when trouble comes.

12. If the success of God's kingdom work in the world depended on the moral fiber of Jesus' disciples, what would be its prospects, and why?

From what you've seen in Mark 14, what does the success of God's work in the world depend on?

RESPONDING TO GOD'S WORD

IN YOUR GROUP:

What trials are your group members undergoing? How can you learn from Jesus how to pray as the James Montgomery hymn,[13] printed below, urges? (If you have access to the Internet, go to the url in the session endnote and listen to the hymn online.)

> *Go to dark Gethsemane, ye that feel the tempter's power;*
> *Your Redeemer's conflict see, watch with Him one bitter hour,*
> *Turn not from His griefs away; learn of Jesus Christ to pray.*
>
> *See Him at the judgment hall, beaten, bound, reviled, arraigned;*
> *O the wormwood and the gall! O the pangs His soul sustained!*
> *Shun not suffering, shame, or loss; learn of Christ to bear the cross.*

Pray for one another.

ON YOUR OWN:

Picture the scene at Gethsemane. Where are you in the scene? Are you one of the sleeping disciples? Are you Jesus? Are you watching Jesus? What do you see and hear? What do you feel? What do you want to say to Jesus or to the Father?

NOTES

1. David J. Garrow, "The FBI and Martin Luther King," *Atlantic Monthly*, July/August 2002, accessed online on July 15, 2009 at *http://www.theatlantic.com/doc/200207/garrow*.
2. Ibid.
3. This section is based on *NIVAC: Mark*, 513–522.
4. This section is based on *NIVAC: Mark*, 523–537.
5. Garland, 526.
6. This section is based on *NIVAC: Mark*, 538–556.
7. Garland, 539.
8. Garland, 539, citing Eduard Schweizer, *The Good News According to Mark* (Richmond, Va.: John Knox, 1970), 311.
9. W. H. Vanstone, *The Stature of Waiting* (New York: Seabury, 1983), 83–85, quoted in Garland, 553–554.
10. This section is based on *NIVAC: Mark*, 557–574.

11. Garland, 562.
12. Garland, 563.
13. James Montgomery, "Go to Dark Gethsemane," in Thomas Cotterill, *Selection of Psalms and Hymns* (London: 1820); quoted in *http://nethymnal.org/htm/g/o/gotodark.htm*, accessed July 15, 2009.

END AND BEGINNING

Mark 15:1–16:8

H ere's a familiar movie plot: Oppressors push a hero to the limit until he can take no more and strikes back. With spectacular violence he takes vengeance until the bad guys are all dead.

This is the story Jesus' followers wanted him to live out. He had the power to do so. Yet he refused. When the evil leaders converged on him, he passively let them do their worst.

Mark knows that someday Jesus will return in power and glory, but Mark lives in dangerous times with no idea when Jesus will come back. Jesus asks Mark — and us — to follow Jesus to the cross, to take the way of servanthood and apparent weakness rather than the way of coercive power. That's not a popular movie plot, because it's not a story we fantasize about living. But like the crowd on Pilate's doorstep, we have to choose: Do we want Jesus or Barabbas?

KING OF THE JEWS[1]

Read Mark 15:1–20.

There was no criminal code for non-Roman citizens tried in the provinces. The Roman governor was free to make rules, to accept or reject charges, and to impose any penalty within reason.

119

He would not have executed a Jew for a religious charge like blasphemy, so the Jewish leaders had to accuse Jesus of treason, of claiming to be a king.

1. It's obvious to Pilate that Jesus is innocent of treason (15:10). Why does Pilate execute a man he can see is innocent?

Pilate has sympathy for Jesus, but he has no intention of paying a price to help him. How is this kind of moral cowardice a temptation today?

Barabbas may have been a freedom fighter against the Romans. Or he may have been a peasant who lost his land through debt and who survived by attacking rich Jewish landlords. There were many such bandits, and to the poor they were Robin Hoods. Barabbas was a Rambo-style hero, a man who fought back violently against his oppressors. Jesus was not.

2. What might the chief priests have said to the crowd (15:11) that made them want to free Barabbas instead of Jesus?

3. What is it about heroes who seek justice by violence that make them seem appealing even to Christians today?

The soldiers mock Jesus because he doesn't fit their idea of what a king should be. "The kings the soldiers have served are those who lord it over others ... who maintain the illusions of power at the expense of others"[2] (cf. 10:42–45). Even today people often prefer leaders like that.

SON OF GOD[3]

Read Mark 15:21–47.

Mark's readers know the gory details of flogging and crucifixion, so Mark doesn't recount them. Instead, he gives only those details about Jesus' torture and death that have theological meaning. And he wants us to hear the irony of what the onlookers say about Jesus.

4. The mockers say that the One who saved others can't save himself (15:31). Their words are truer than they know. Why can't Jesus save both himself and others?

The many ways Jesus' death fulfills Old Testament predictions shows that his "end is not a tragic failure but the glorious fulfillment of the destiny God assigned him as the Messiah."[4] In particular, Jesus calls attention to Psalm 22 by crying out its first verse (15:34).

5. Compare Mark 15:24–34 to Psalm 22:1–18. What echoes of the psalm do you find in Mark's account?

Read Psalm 22:23–31. What does the end of this psalm tell you about the destiny Jesus expects even as he quotes the beginning of the psalm in anguish?

6. When faced with the worst suffering, Jesus prays a psalm that expresses anguish and complaint, but also trust in God. What can we learn for our own lives from the way Jesus faced death?

As the heavens were torn open at the beginning of Jesus' ministry (Mark 1:10), so the temple curtain is torn open at the end (15:38). This curtain separated the temple's court and Holy Place (which one Jewish writer compared to the land and sea, accessible to humanity) from the Holy of Holies (which represented heaven, the dwelling place of God). The temple is now obsolete, for Jesus has fulfilled its purpose. The barrier between humanity and God is torn away, and God's glory floods out into the world.

7. What implications does the tearing of the temple curtain have for us?

8. Like the soldiers who mocked Jesus (15:16–20), the centurion who watches Jesus die (15:39) has been taught to call Caesar alone the Son of God. Caesar proves his divinity by wielding naked power. What do you think it is about Jesus' death that convinces this hardened military man to shift his thinking and call Jesus the Son of God?

GOING DEEPER

The centurion is the opposite of the people who want to see dramatic proof before believing (15:36). "Faith is not a matter of seeing in order to believe, but of trusting to the point of death."[5] One must be able to see that precisely here in the obscurity, lowliness, humiliation, and powerlessness of the cross, not in any miraculous display, God demonstrates power over the demonic and humankind.[6]

9. What does the cross tell us about God?

THE RISEN LORD[7]

Read Mark 16:1–8.

Before the crucifixion, Mark never mentioned Jesus' women followers, but now they surface as the primary witnesses to Jesus' death (15:40–41), burial (15:47), and resurrection. There's evidence that Jewish law didn't recognize women as legal witnesses, but as he often does, God chooses and dignifies those whom others dismiss as insignificant. These women can't buy burial spices or travel on the Sabbath, but they take action as soon as they can.

10. Mark shows no joyful reunion of Jesus with either his male or female followers. He gives us only the angel's terse announcement in 16:6 ("he has risen") and instruction in 16:7 ("go, tell"). Like these women, we have to trust the claim that "he has risen" without seeing Jesus with our own eyes. Why should we believe the angel's message without the proof of seeing Jesus physically?

11. Initially, the women fail to obey the command to go and tell (16:7), because they're scared (v. 8). What do you think they are afraid of?

Why are we sometimes afraid to go and tell that Jesus has risen?

Mark's book ends with the promise that Jesus is going ahead of his disciples, leading the way as he has always done (16:7), even though his disciples are confused and frightened, and consistently fail him (16:8). Later scribes tacked on extra endings beyond verse 8,[8] endings that wrap things up more neatly by taking scenes from the other gospels. But Mark probably intended to leave the story open-ended, because for him this is only "The beginning of the good news" (1:1), and it's up to Jesus' disciples to carry the good news forward by following where he leads.

12. Mark's abrupt ending leaves it to us to take the next step in the story. What step of faith is your study of Mark's gospel calling you to take?

RESPONDING TO GOD'S WORD

IN YOUR GROUP:

Mark believes absolutely in the resurrection, but he doesn't want triumphal scenes of it to obscure the terrifying scandal of the cross. He wants us not simply to sing about how we survey the wondrous cross, glory in the cross, or love the old rugged cross. He wants us to become like Jesus in obedience and live the cross. Pray as honestly as you can about what this might mean for each of you and how you feel about it.

> Lord Jesus, it's scary for us to stand before hostile people and speak of you as King of Kings and Son of God. We don't want to be mocked, let alone physically abused, as the soldiers, the chief priests, and even the criminals mocked you. It's natural for us to hate being ridiculed, to hate pain, to hate weakness and humiliation. A part of each of our hearts is drawn to Barabbas-style leaders who fight back against evil instead of

paying the price to overcome evil with good. But we do believe you are the King, the Son of God, the risen Lord who has defeated evil and death and who goes before us. Please help our unbelief, cure our blind spots, and give us courage. For Caesar is not Lord; you are the only Lord worth following. In the power of your name we pray, Amen.

This is a somber note on which to end a group study. You might plan some extra refreshments to celebrate having completed this journey with Mark together and to discuss where you go from here.

ON YOUR OWN:

Pray slowly through Psalm 22. The first time through, try to picture this as Jesus' prayer. Picture him on the cross, and try to imagine what he feels as he suffers and prays. Then pray through it again. Can you imagine yourself being in such a place and saying these things to God? Which parts of the psalm speak most deeply of what is in you?

NOTES

1. This section is based on *NIVAC: Mark*, 575–584.
2. Garland, 581–582.
3. This section is based on *NIVAC: Mark*, 585–609.
4. Garland, 593.
5. Frank J. Matera, *Passion Narratives and Gospel Theologies* (New York/Mahwah, N.J.: Paulist Press, 1986), 44, quoted in Garland, 605.
6. Garland, 605.
7. This section is based on *NIVAC: Mark*, 610–630.
8. The earliest and most reliable manuscripts end with verse 8.

LEADER'S NOTES

SESSION 1 LEADER'S NOTES

1. Jesus comes to fulfill divine promises and his own divine commission. He is greater than the prophet John and will baptize with God's Holy Spirit.

2. John is God's messenger to prepare the way for Jesus' earthly ministry. Jesus is the Father's messenger sent to his disciples and to us, to prepare the way, the road on which we are to follow him. "As the story unfolds, Jesus leads the disciples on the way to Jerusalem and death (10:32), and he goes before them to Galilee (14:28; 16:7)."[1] "The 'way' (*hodos*; 1:2) appears again as a theme in 8:27; 9:33–34; 10:32, 52. . . . The way for him will end in Jerusalem and in a solitary death. . . . Jesus is the one who must be out in front, blazing the trail. . . . Disciples are those who follow in his way (8:34–10:52)."[2]

3. Some of us (especially women) are uncomfortable with the word *power*. But we still strive to achieve, to use our abilities, to influence, to have freedom to do what we want. These are all exercises of power, and it's important to be honest with ourselves about that. Power doesn't have to be power *over* others; it can be power *for* others. Both the means and the goals of using power can be good or bad. For instance, manipulation and subtle control are as much abuses of power as is direct force.

   "One might . . . assume that the Messiah, the Son of God, would cut a more imposing figure, who would immediately capture the attention of the crowds. Instead, this Messiah, the one who comes from No-wheres-ville in rustic Galilee, seems indistinguishable from the rest of the crowds. He does not come with some special aura or halo."[3] His exercise of power on behalf of others, not for self-glorification, shows us both the goals and the means of using power that he wants us to imitate.

4. The narrator tells us who Jesus is: God's Son, God's beloved. "One can interpret the voice at Jesus' baptism as God's announcement that Jesus has been chosen to rule over his people and that he assumes royal power as king. This enthronement, however, is private; and the reader may wonder when others will recognize and accept him as king."[4] We are forced to ask ourselves: If Jesus is truly king, then how can we live as his subjects?

5. Sojourning with wild animals may seem idyllic to us, but one of the ways Nero martyred Christians was by letting wild animals tear them up while an audience watched. For Mark's readers, wild animals meant danger. But led by the Spirit, Jesus overcame both the spiritual attack of Satan and the physical danger of animals. As Mark goes on to show Jesus facing unclean spirits and threats to his life, we know from his time in the wilderness that he has already decisively defeated Satan and overcome threats to his physical safety.

6. Jesus appears so successful, a golden boy. He heals and teaches with authority. It's easy to get caught up in the celebrity moment if we forget (as Jesus never did) that he is all the while heading toward death.

7. As leader, think about this question ahead of time, and be prepared to tell what having Jesus as king, rather than yourself, involves for you.

8. "[T]hese men show their repentance, their desire 'to turn,' by dropping everything to heed Jesus' call. Their repentance is more than just a matter of an internal transformation; they turn into something that they are not now, from fishermen to fishers of men."[5]

"Jesus is going somewhere and requires his disciples to come along with him (1:18; 2:14; 10:21). He does not call them to attend endless seminars on discipleship training with lively discussions on the theological fine points of the law. Discipleship in Mark is not about mastering theoretical ideas; it is about mission, a common mission with Jesus (6:7, 30)."[6]

9. "Mark wants to underscore the force of Jesus' call. It alone propels [the disciples] to follow him. He chooses whom he wills, and his call comes like 'a sharp military command' that produces obedience."[7]

10. The power to drive out the anti-God forces demonstrates Jesus' authority to teach what God says.

11. For example, Jesus' desire for secluded prayer shows that he is "not a sorcerer working by magic independent of God's help. His authority, strength, and power come from God alone (see 9:29)."[8] Also, he is constantly traveling to preach the kingdom. And the healing of the leper underscores his compassion, even for those whom society scorns. Leprosy was seen as a punishment for sin, and people believed only God could heal it, so Jesus' power over it is as remarkable as his power over demons.

12. Whenever someone disobeys Jesus' command for silence, the next scene starts with a reference to the crushing crowds, hindering his free movement and pushing him to be a celebrity rather than a herald of God's kingdom. We today can be distracted by the allure of approval and success, and confuse these with obedience to God.

13. We might as well admit that Jesus' call is as daunting as it is exhilarating. "Disciples are not those who simply fill pews at worship, fill out pledge cards, attend an occasional Bible study, and offer to help out in the work of the church now and then. They are not merely eavesdroppers and onlookers. When one is hooked by Jesus, one's whole life and purpose in life are transformed."[9] Discipleship is risky and gets in the way of pursuing money and success. "What keeps us from this full commitment is a fatal illusion that our real needs are physical, and it results in our self-centered concern for material security. But Jesus is not only able to deliver people from the bondage of unclean spirits and disease, he can deliver us from bondage to material concerns (such as the desire to preserve our standard of living at all costs). He gives us a vision that there is more to life than catching a string of fish. The center of life is to revolve around God. The authority of his call dispels our hesitancy and awakens total confidence in God. Disciples are the ones who throw caution to the winds."[10]

NOTES

1. Garland, 45.
2. Garland, 56.
3. Garland, 47.
4. Garland, 49.
5. Garland, 69.

6. Garland, 86.
7. Garland, 78
8. Garland, 73.
9. Garland, 84.
10. Garland, 85.

SESSION 2 LEADER'S NOTES

1. As in 1:25–27, Jesus' acts of authority raise questions. But while the earlier people marvel and really want to know what is happening, the teachers of the law are merely angry. Their question "why" doesn't really seek an honest explanation. Jesus doesn't fit their theology, and they aren't open to something new.

2. "Will someone who has to be carried in on a pallet by others believe Jesus' word about the forgiveness of his sins to act on his directive to get up and carry it out? Or, will he accept the judgment of the teachers of the law and say to himself: 'This man cannot forgive my sins'? Will he convince himself that this is a hopeless command?"[1]

3. It's extremely hard to think outside our theological boxes. It requires humility and openness to new information, a genuine willingness to be proved wrong and to learn. For Jesus, it's a matter of how hard or soft a person's heart is. Or as the parable says in Mark 4, what kind of soil for planting seeds their heart is.

4. The Pharisees are right in understanding that only God can forgive sins, and that a man can't just dismiss sin effortlessly. Sin is horrible, and there is a price that must be paid. But they don't know who Jesus is, or what he will do about sin on the cross that allows him to forgive it without minimizing its seriousness. On the cross Jesus will "give his life as a ransom for many" (10:45), paying the price that frees them from sin and its penalty.

5. Jesus' acts of healing and forgiveness change "the questions that are normally asked when suffering or misfortune strikes. Instead of asking, 'Who did this to me?' or 'Why did this happen?' one needs to ask, 'Who is this who offers forgiveness, healing, and salvation?' and 'What does his presence in our lives mean?'"[2]

6. "[F]ollowing Jesus is open to 'all-comers.' One's position or caste, even one's shady reputation, is not a liability when it comes to receiving and responding to Jesus' call."[3]

7. Some of these "sinners" may simply be ordinary people disliked by the Pharisees because they don't follow the Pharisees' views on how to live holy lives, because they associate with Gentiles, or because they practice a blacklisted trade, such as tanning leather that required contact with dead

animals. Also, "to follow Jesus in the full sense of the word requires repentance and obedience. His goal in reaching out to the sick [and sinful] is to bring about healing and transformation in their lives, not to gather them together for a fun time."[4]

8. The central question for us is whether we believe that radical moral transformation is possible, and whether our churches know how to help people undergo radical transformation. If churches have no idea how to do this, it often seems safer to settle for keeping nice middle-class youth and adults out of trouble. If we think it's more likely that our kids will be "infected" by the sins of troubled kids than that troubled kids will be infected by the robust godliness of our kids, then we tend to focus on protecting our own rather than reaching out to others.

9. If we see Christian living as mainly about preserving our purity, then we tend to look at others as potential polluters of our purity. But Jesus rejects this view. See if you can help group members talk about what makes social outcasts uncomfortable to Christians. For instance: Such people often smell of smoke. They may be dirty. They may drink. They may use foul language. They may look hardened or promiscuous. They may make fun of our faith.

10. Christian worship should be marked by joy, although that doesn't exclude times of grieving, either grieving over suffering or grieving over our sins. The wineskins signify the newness of life in God's kingdom as opposed to the previous regime. Pre-Jesus Judaism, as fine as it was in some ways, is obsolete because of Jesus.

11. The Pharisees think the Sabbath rules about not working mean that if a person doesn't already have food prepared, he should go hungry, and if he is sick, he should wait a day for treatment. Christians, too, can create rules that effectively cut them off from redemptive involvement with non-Christians.

12. We can pray for God to show us our stubbornness and blind spots. We can ask others to help us see these things, and we can refrain from anger when someone tells us.

NOTES

1. Garland, 95.
2. Garland, 98.
3. Garland, 104.
4. Ibid.

1. Jesus heals and teaches the crowd, but he takes his disciples away for deeper teaching and personal contact with him. He also gives the Twelve authority to do the miraculous things he has been doing and to proclaim the kingdom as he has.

2. The disciples had to deal with crushing crowds that kept them even from eating. They had to go out and do the hard work of preaching the kingdom. They had to endure increasing hostility from respected members of their society. For us, the hard part of being with Jesus may be that he takes time away from our pursuit of money, career, and social standing. He may call us into contact with people who make us uncomfortable. He may ask us to trust him to provide for us. He may bring us into conflict with people we'd prefer to appease.

3. Jesus' family are those people who do his will. The bonds between disciples will be stronger than blood ties.

4. So far, Jesus has shown that doing God's will involves repentance, spending time with him, pursuing a greater understanding of him, getting involved with people who don't live pure religious lives, caring for those oppressed by sickness and evil, and proclaiming the kingdom. And there is more to come.

5. The crowds would say Jesus is an amazing healer and teacher from whom one might get something desirable if one hangs around. The demons would say he's the Holy One of God, to be exposed or avoided. The disciples might say he's a great teacher worth following even at some personal cost. Jesus' family fears he's crazy. The teachers of the law think he's a dangerous fraud to be stopped.

6. The teachers of the law are like the path, so hard that the seed doesn't even begin to penetrate.

7. A genuine question shows humility (we don't have all the answers) as well as a desire to learn from Jesus. It shows we are not indifferent to his teaching. Less fruitful responses are hostility, or believing we understand everything, or embracing Jesus happily but then going on with life without pursuing him consistently, or embracing his teaching until life gets hard or following him costs us something.

8. Jesus promises that suffering will be part of the normal Christian life. "The good hearer welcomes the word immediately so that it cannot be snatched away by Satan. The good hearer welcomes it deeply so that it is not withered by persecution. The good hearer welcomes it exclusively so that other concerns do not strangle it."[1]

9. We need to pray against and choose against relentless desire for other things, including material things. In Christian communities we need to reinforce less consumption rather than give extra honor to those who have the nicest houses and clothes. "[I]n our consumer-oriented society, a faith that calls for sacrifice and service for others soon takes a back seat.... The glut of how-to books flooding the market, which promise to teach the buyers how to relax their way to success, to be energetic and beautiful, to win big money, unlimited power, and control over others, reveals that we live in a narcissistic age."[2] We need to stand against this because it chokes the word, making our lives unfruitful.

10. Sometimes we don't want to know more about Jesus because we're afraid of what we might learn about ourselves. And most of us also know someone like this. Talk about how we can overcome such obstacles and help others to do so too.

11. We need to avoid prejudging outsiders. The sower casts seeds without deciding ahead of time whether the soil has potential. We need to be in relationships even with people who seem unpromising. And keeping insiders safe is less important than training them to live the gospel in a dangerous world. We need to teach the whole gospel, "including the discomforting parts that hack away at our selfish concerns to be at ease and uplifted—and let whatever happens happen."[3]

12. Sowing the word is an essential, not an optional, part of the Christian life. Many of us avoid it because we hate rejection and failure. "Frequently people judge success by numbers. Americans in particular assume that bigger is better and that the presence of large numbers is a sure sign of the Spirit's presence. The corollary is that failure is also measured by numbers, and a low response is construed as a sign of the Spirit's absence. The danger of these assumptions for the spiritual development of disciples is that we will offer the lowest common denominator spirituality, which caters to mass appeal and fails to challenge the hearers' sins and worldviews."[4]

NOTES

1. Garland, 164.
2. Garland, 172.
3. Garland, 170.
4. Garland, 169–170.

SESSION 4 LEADER'S NOTES

1. Jesus is like a lamp for those in darkness, yet instead of making his identity and teaching obvious, he veils them. This seems as strange as putting a lamp under a bowl. "God's glory is revealed indirectly in disarming ways through riddling parables, weakness, suffering, and death. The mystery of the relationship of Jesus to God's reign will become clearer after his death on the cross and his resurrection—after his earthly ministry—but even then it will go unrecognized by those who grope in their own darkness."[1] The one who snubs Jesus has everything to lose; "the one who risks faith in what now lies hidden has everything to gain."[2]

2. "Can one believe that the kingdom of God advances through ignominy, through defeat, through crucifixion?... During the sowing stage, the beginning of the gospel (1:1), one must make a leap of faith that what Jesus says about himself and God's kingdom is true.... The final stage will reveal a dramatic change from the beginning, but by then it will be too late for those who were unable to see what God was doing all along."[3]

3. Onlookers need to trust that the tiny seed will produce something magnificent. But the process takes time, and we can't control it. This calls for long patience.

4. "We live in the in-between time, between the beginning when the seed is sown and the end time when the final stage becomes manifest and all God's purposes are accomplished."[4] We shouldn't get discouraged or look to something that seems more secure or promising. Also, "Sometimes our frenetic activity may be a smoke screen that hides our lack of trust in God. We feel we need to take control before God's will can be done. The parable allows us to stop concentrating on what we need to accomplish or have accomplished and to reflect on what God is accomplishing. It encourages us to trust the seed to do what seeds do in the soil."[5]

5. Jesus so trusts in God's protection that he can be completely relaxed. He is a model for his disciples of faith that means trust in God.

6. "Jesus' explanation of his parables did not prepare them for anything as portentous as this miracle.... The disciples' fear stems from Jesus' God-like control of the sea (see Ps. 89:9).... The disciples' awe before the numinous is appropriate, but they still have only the vaguest inkling of who this

man is in their midst, who wields such power. The light may be too bright for their eyes to take it all in."[6]

7. The man "has been beaten and chained by others and now lashes himself with stones in a desperate attempt to purge himself of his inner turmoil. The legion of unclean spirits causes the possessed man to race toward Jesus and prostrate himself before him (5:6) in a desperate bid to ward off an exorcism."[7] The spirits try to overpower Jesus by speaking his name. They try to distract and then negotiate with him.

8. The Gerasenes want Jesus to leave before he destroys any more businesses. "They are more comfortable with the malevolent forces that take captive human beings and destroy animals than they are with the one who can expel them.... This benighted community becomes another example of the outsiders who see but do not see.... They chase off the source of their deliverance and salvation. People can tolerate religion as long as it does not affect business profits."[8]

9. The woman is afraid when she knows she's been healed. Jesus' power frightens her as it frightened the disciples on the lake. Jairus is afraid that Jesus might not be powerful enough.

10. The woman and Jairus both have to trust in the midst of hopelessness. She has to risk exposure and have the faith to engage in relationship with Jesus; he has to risk disappointment and ridicule. "Faith opens the door to the power of God. Faith transfers divine power to those who are utterly powerless.... Faith can be imperfect; it can be bold; it can be halting; it can be brave; it can be laced with fear and trepidation. What counts for it to be effective is for it to be directed rightly to Jesus and God."[9]

11. Jesus has God's power. Comparing Mark's stories with Isaiah 43:1–10 shows that Mark sees Jesus as doing what only God can do. Jesus is God in the flesh. He comes to heal and rescue. He comes for relationship. He comes for those of both high and low status. He is unpredictable and defies our demand to perform on our schedule. He values trust.

12. Do you want the Jesus of the calmed storm, exorcism, and physical healings without the Jesus of hiddenness, patience, and suffering? If so, you may be in danger of rejecting him as his fellow villagers did.

NOTES

1. Garland, 175.
2. Garland, 176.
3. Garland, 179–180.
4. Garland, 184.
5. Garland, 187.
6. Garland, 193.
7. Garland, 190.
8. Garland, 206.
9. Garland, 227.

1. "To go on mission entirely dependent on the generosity of others for food and lodging is an expression of extreme poverty. They do not travel first class. They do not come like an invading army living off the land. The Twelve come more humbly and must be totally dependent on God for their support. They are to go out as the poor to those who are also poor and hungry.... 'Weakness and poverty are effective means of proclaiming that men should repent (1 Cor. 2:3–5).'"[1]

2. Although a decision is necessary, sometimes we may be too quick to push people to decide for Christ. We need to give them a chance to think through something that may be entirely foreign to the way they were raised. They need a chance to work through their emotional barriers as well as their intellectual ones. On the other hand, it does matter that they come to know who Jesus is. We need to feel both urgency and extreme patience.

3. If we feel overwhelmed by the size of the need, we may need to think back to the parables about sowing seeds. We need do only our tiny part and trust God for results—but we do need to do our part and not be lazy. "The disciples' mission is not just a matter of preaching the good news but of bringing into effect in people's lives the good news of healing and deliverance. They do not offer people something new to believe in but something that tangibly changes their lives. The good news is not just about saving souls but is also connected to physical healing" and restoration.[2]

4. Just as John is "handed over," so Jesus will be. "Just as John is executed by a reluctant political ruler at the instigation of a conniving individual who plotted his death behind the scenes (6:14–29), so Jesus will be sentenced to death by a reluctant political ruler at the instigation of hostile leaders who engineer his death behind the scenes (14:1–2; 15:1–2, 11). Just as Herodias seized an 'opportune time' to carry out her evil designs (6:21), so Judas will seek an 'opportunity' to betray Jesus to the high priests (14:11). Just as Herod was caught off guard by the response to his reckless offer (6:23–26), so Pilate will be surprised by the response to his offer of releasing a prisoner (15:6–15)."[3]

5. "The power to do miracles does not grant [Jesus' followers] immunity from suffering and death."[4] True gospel ministry is unlikely to be all glamour and no suffering. Those who proclaim the gospel should expect hatred and retaliation from some, and curiosity but ultimately nonresponse from others. These are two kinds of bad soil in which the seed may be sown. Yet despite the dangers and rejection, sowers sow anyway because there will be a harvest. We needn't be cynical, and we mustn't retreat.

6. The people's hunger really is physical, but it also points to their spiritual hunger.

7. God is the source of nourishment for all of our deepest needs, whether of body or spirit. God cares, God responds, and God has plenty.

8. In this story, Jesus acts as the shepherd who truly cares for the sheep (6:34). He makes them sit down, like sheep lying down in green pastures. He restores their souls with teaching. He prepares a banquet for them despite their enemies, the Romans, occupying their country.

9. "This incident also emphasizes the need to combine teaching with social concern. As God did not neglect the physical and spiritual needs of the people of Israel in the desert, so the church cannot neglect either need. Jesus provides the bread of life. He offers the people bread that feeds the soul and bread that satisfies the needs of the body. On the one hand, giving Bible lessons to large crowds and sending them away hungry does too little. Starving people rarely make good religious followers because they are intent on physical survival. On the other hand, simply filling their bellies without also filling their hearts with a spiritual challenge does too little. The two go hand in hand."[5]

10. The disciples see only something that looks to them like a ghost. It terrifies them. When Jesus speaks to them and they realize it's him, they're astounded, shaken. They can't get their minds around his ability to do things that go way beyond what even a miracle-working prophet could do. Only God can tread on waves. He is revealing himself as God, and they can't fathom it.

11. The disciples are blind to this revelation of God as a man. "The condition of hardened hearts refers to disobedience, dullness, and obstinacy and is the predicament of Jesus' opponents (3:5; see Eph. 4:18)."[6] Awe before something holy and Other is the appropriate response.

12. This is a chance to share personal experiences, to see God at work in your lives, and to be encouraged by other followers of Jesus.

NOTES

1. Garland, 241.
2. Garland, 249.
3. Garland, 246.
4. Garland, 247.
5. Garland, 258.
6. Garland, 265.

1. The Pharisees' traditions are only man-made. Their hearts are too often not involved. And sometimes their man-made traditions actually keep them from obeying biblical commands. For instance, they put the keeping of vows ahead of the commandment to honor parents. Jesus thinks that priority order is dead wrong.

2. Jesus isn't against tradition. There are many valuable Christian traditions and much to learn from believers in past generations and centuries, so we don't need to reinvent the wheel in every decade. Jesus isn't encouraging novelty.

3. For instance, it might be possible to tithe in the manner your church prescribes and yet have your heart far away from helping others with your resources.

4. For instance, many churches urge members to avoid getting involved with unbelievers who have sinful practices that may contaminate them. But most unbelievers have sinful practices, so this desire for purity can effectively cut us off from caring for the broken people around us.

5. Moral impurity comes from within, from the heart, so it can't be washed off with any kind of ceremonial ritual.

6. We need to focus on the transformation of motives, habits of thought, and other matters of the heart. We need to examine why we do what we do. Discipleship that focuses on controlling outward behavior is misguided. Attending to inner transformation will lead to changes in behavior, because behavior flows from the heart.

7. Jesus has come first to the Jews. They are his priority during his earthly ministry. He himself is the bread that gives life. And yes, he refers to Gentiles as "dogs," just as most Jews would in his day. He wants to see how this woman will respond to such insulting language. (He calls Jews "this adulterous and sinful generation" in 8:38, so he's not singling out the Gentiles for strong words!)

8. "The woman shows the greatest humility that expels her prejudice when she begs for a few crumbs from the bread sent to the Jews. She does not become caustic or bitter about the privilege of others. She does not resent their share of God's blessing. She accepts her place and comes, as everyone

must, as a sinner, poor and needy. Dwight Moody is reported to have said that Jesus sent no one away empty except those who were full of themselves. She may have been a Gentile idolater, but she did not suffer from I-dolatry. She did not come expecting praise for her faith but wanting healing for her sick daughter. She accepts that she is unacceptable. Jesus' ministry reveals that God has not sent him to reward the deserving but to serve the needy, whoever they are and wherever they may be found. God helps those who confess that they are needy and deserve nothing."[1]

9. Are we able to be as humble as this woman, or are we I-dolaters? Do we need Jesus to stroke our self-esteem, or are we desperate for him?

10. "Jesus is now offering a predominantly Gentile crowd the same opportunity to be fed by his teaching and by his miraculous power that he offered to the Jewish crowd. We may think that it is only fair that Gentiles get a share in Christ's benefits, but from Mark's Jewish perspective the inclusion of Gentiles is a token of the end-time reign of God. The miracle signifies that Jesus is not simply '*a* redeemer, *a* messiah like Moses and David'; he is *the* Redeemer, offering redemption to more than just the people of Israel."[2]

11. The disciples should understand that Jesus *himself* is all the bread they need, as he is the source of unlimited bread, both physical and spiritual. They must not fall victim to the insidious leaven-like unbelief of the Pharisees and Herodians. They must not be obsessed with where their next meal is coming from but should trust Jesus. But they don't understand precisely because their hearts are hard—and will be hard until after the resurrection.

12. Jesus wants the kind of humility and faith that pursues him in desperation, like the pagan woman's. He doesn't care about his society's social boundaries. He has bread to offer, but if we're preoccupied like the disciples, we won't ask and receive.

13. This is a chance to share your own needs and receive prayer in the group.

NOTES

1. Garland, 296.
2. D. W. Chapman, *The Orphan Gospel: Mark's Perspective on Jesus*, The Biblical Seminar 16 (Sheffield, England: JSOT, 1993), 66, quoted in Garland, 307.

SESSION 7 LEADER'S NOTES

1. Peter understands what the crowd doesn't. Jesus is not just a prophet; he is the Messiah.

2. Peter still thinks the Messiah will be a triumphant military leader, not a king who gains victory through humiliation and death. Nothing that Peter has been taught about the Messiah allows him to think of a Messiah who endures what Jesus describes.

3. Peter is tempting Jesus to avoid the suffering that will lead to sin's defeat and to give in to selfish desires. He's tempting Jesus to turn away from God's plan for the Messiah.

4. Jesus has put aside the normal life, with its desires for a wife and children, as well as ambition for success and long life. He has poured himself out in service to others, and he will do that to the utter end. He has also lived without yielding to the temptation of sin.

5. Our society preaches self-actualization and self-fulfillment, not self-denial. It confuses the self-denial Jesus speaks of with a distorted form that tells people to be passive doormats with no desires—and no courage to follow Jesus either. Jesus is talking about brave, active, forward-moving self-denial. If we find it scary, we're normal. Not many will be called upon to give up their lives in martyrdom. But all who follow Christ must practice the painful form of self-denial by not giving in to those powerful temptations that would lead to sin. It is better to suffer self-denial than to sin.

6. Take some time to think this through. Group members may not have easy answers and may need to reflect on this.

7. We may try to save our lives by seeking approval from people. We may do it by pouring ourselves into careers or trying to raise perfect children. We may even do it by wearing ourselves out with church work. Even activities that are good in themselves can be forms of self-indulgence that cause us to lose our lives if they draw us away from dependence on the source of life: Jesus.

8. For instance, Christians can get caught up in triumphalist fantasies of worshiping and ministering at big, successful, influential churches; winning political battles; or making money. Like Peter, we're drawn dangerously to power, not weakness and suffering.

9. We need to be confident of Christ's glorious victory over death in order to endure the cross with him. This glimpse gives us courage and hope. But we must not demand the triumph now so that we can escape the cross.

10. Jesus is talking about consistent prayer and total dependence on God. There are no techniques that are keys to getting God to do what we want; there are no right words; nor do we need to drum up the psychological state of strong belief. Jesus prays consistently throughout Mark's gospel. The disciples fail to heal because they aren't dependent on Jesus but want power for themselves. They lack the humility and faith needed to minister in the name of the Lord.

11. "We may get the impression from Mark 4:40 and 6:6 that doubt and faith are mutually exclusive: Either one has faith, or one is stuck in the morass of unbelief. This father's plea, 'I do believe; help me overcome my unbelief,' and Jesus' commands to have faith (5:36) reveal a paradox about faith that most believers experience. As [Christopher] Marshall states it, 'There is within every believer a tension between faith and unfaith, and that faith can only continue to exist by dint of divine aid.' ... This father tethers what little faith he has to Christ and asks for help just as he is. Jesus does not expect him to summon up a mighty faith before anything can be done but only to trust that God can act decisively through him."[1]

12. Here is a chance to share your own tension between faith and unfaith, and the situations that trigger that tension in you.

NOTE

1. Garland, 363.

SESSION 8 LEADER'S NOTES

1. The key to achieving greatness in the Lord's work is to put oneself last and be the servant of all. And there's often a price to pay when we try to counteract a "self-important, self-admiring, and self-glorious spirit within a church ... because those tainted with it wield their power with determination. Only those who exude a loving and humble spirit themselves and are willing to take the consequences will be able to challenge and help others who imperiously try to throw their weight around."[1]

2. If we want to be great in God's eyes, then these vulnerable, disrespected ones are the ones we are to single out for attention. Whoever cares for those who are vulnerable and ignored is welcoming Jesus himself, and the Father.

3. You may have no ministry involvement with people of low status, but you may employ them, see them working in restaurants, or see them on the streets. If they are completely invisible to you, consider making a point of looking for them for the next few weeks. Ask God, "What is mine to do for these people?"

4. "For some today, turning off the television would be as bad as plucking out an eye. One must be careful about the answer to this question. We may dull the saying's sharp edge so much that no one takes notice.... Jesus, however, deliberately chose harsh, scandalous imagery to alert disciples that their lives tremble in the balance.... [A] lackadaisical disregard for sin in one's own life imperils one's salvation."[2]

5. Marriage is rooted in how humans are designed. It's not something societies create and can reinvent at will. It comes from how God has created us. We are intended to become one flesh with one other person for life. Hard-heartedness happens, and we need to grapple realistically with it, but breaking the one-flesh relationship is a serious matter.

6. Most marital problems could be dealt with if both partners were committed to being one another's servants rather than seeking the upper hand and the fulfillment of selfish desires. A marriage might be saved if one partner commits to this, although it will be painful for that partner. The issues in deeply troubled marriages are usually quite complex. Couples should seek assistance from their pastor or other spiritual counselors.

7. "What [Jesus] might have said ... we can only surmise from what he said to the woman caught in adultery (John 7:53 – 8:11) and to the Samaritan woman who had five husbands and was living with a man who was not her husband (4:4 – 29)."[3] Certainly, if one is still married, adopting a posture of forgiveness and servanthood is the best course. But in cases of physical abuse, separation, if not divorce, is often advisable. Sometimes people have to decide which is the least evil course while not pretending that divorce is good. Those who are already divorced must understand that divorce is not the unforgivable sin, and relearn the fundamentals of marriage and relationships from Scripture.

8. Jesus tells the man to go, sell everything, give to the poor, and follow him. As he doesn't tell all prosperous people to sell everything they have, he probably asks this particular man to do so because he depends too heavily on his wealth as his source of well-being and security. But many of us might fall into that category too. The radical nature of Jesus' command expresses how serious this issue is.

9. "[I]f one wants eternal life, everything depends on one's response to Jesus."[4] Giving all to the poor doesn't do it. Obeying and following Jesus does it. The invitation to follow is unearned grace, but responding can be costly.

10. This is a scary question. Consider your schedule. Christians often say they are too busy to build relationships with non-Christians in order to offer them the gospel, and too busy to serve the poor. But what we are busy with is often working to acquire money and then spending money to acquire possessions and maintain our home. If maintaining our lifestyles is so time-consuming that we don't have time to do the work of the gospel, then what? There are no easy answers.

11. We're left with grace, total dependence on God's unearned kindness to do for us what we can't do for ourselves.

12. It's painful and frustrating to subordinate our desires to serve others, who are often not remotely grateful. The cost of giving up status-seeking is that we have to endure others looking down on us. This is impossible to sustain long term unless we are connected to Jesus as the source of life and love, as the One who made that life available to us by dying. "The only way that disciples can possibly live up to Jesus' demands is to realize that he has gone before them, broken through, and cleared the way for others to

follow. He is like the man who cut the path through the jungle for days in order to lead a group of prisoners back to freedom and life and then died of exhaustion upon arrival.... They were with him on this march; yet he was the only one who was strong enough to open the way, and he died in doing so."[5]

NOTES

1. Garland, 371–372.
2. Garland, 374.
3. Garland, 391.
4. Garland, 396.
5. Garland, 415.

SESSION 9 LEADER'S NOTES

1. Jesus has come to Jerusalem to die, so he is ready to draw fire. He's ready to be acclaimed as king, because he's about to demonstrate what his kingship means. Yet his entry isn't triumphal. He doesn't enter Jerusalem on a white charger as a conquering power. He comes peacefully and humbly.

2. Jesus is the Lord (God) coming to his temple. He is the messenger of God's covenant. Like refining fire, he will purify a people through suffering, as he himself will suffer. He "enters the temple to inspect it, and the next day's events reveal that he comes not to restore it but to pronounce God's judgment on it."[1]

   Like the crowds, we may like to greet the Messiah with rejoicing, but we need to avoid a too-triumphal attitude. Jesus will come again someday in power and glory, but for now we walk with him to the cross, and we need to be saved from a fair-weather faith that abandons him at the first sign of trouble.

3. Jesus "trains his sights on three things: the fiscal foundation of the temple, a vital component of its sacrifices, and a crucial element of its liturgy. If money cannot be exchanged into the holy currency, then monetary support for the temple sacrifices and the priesthood must end. If sacrificial animals cannot be purchased, then sacrifice must end. If no vessel can be carried through the temple, then all cultic activity must cease. Jesus does not seek to purify current temple worship but symbolically attacks the very function of the temple and heralds its destruction."[2] He is about to replace it with his own self-sacrifice.

4. Jesus' sacrifice enables us to sin and receive forgiveness. But if we want to sin persistently, are we really true disciples? Are we perhaps deluding ourselves that believing some things about him is enough for salvation? Saving faith means trusting and following him. Disciples struggle with sin, hate their sin. They aren't blasé about it.

5. Jesus is talking about faith *in God*, not in ourselves or our dreams. "Prayer is not imposing our will on God but opening up our lives to God's will. True prayer is not an endeavor to get God to change his will but an endeavor to release that will in our own lives."[3] Prayer isn't a magic wand that lets us get whatever we want. Jesus wants us to pray confidently

(because nothing is impossible for him) but not with bravado. What we ask "must be compatible with his teaching, life, and death."[4]

6. Hostility toward others closes our hearts and pushes God away from working in that relationship.

7. The leaders in Jerusalem are the tenants of God's vineyard. They killed the past prophets, and they are about to kill God's Son. Jesus clearly claims to be God's Son with foreknowledge of his death. That the leaders "move ahead with their plot means that they carry it out with malice aforethought."[5]

8. We followers of Christ are the new temple where God dwells (see 1 Peter 2:2–5). We should think of ourselves not as a myriad of individual temples, but as one temple together. We are thus connected to each other and can only be "a house of prayer for all nations" when we are united under the lordship of Christ.

9. We are made in God's image. To give him what is his is to give him our whole selves, body and soul. We don't owe him 10 percent of our income; we owe him everything—all our time and money, all our energy and life.

10. Most of the time we are to obey our government (Rom. 13:1–7). But we need to oppose unjust laws and to discern when laws are too unjust to obey.

11. Many people believe that all but the worst of us will go to heaven, a place of disembodied pleasantness. Others believe we are repeatedly reincarnated into new bodies born on this earth until we receive enlightenment and escape the cycle of rebirth. Others believe we altogether cease to exist after death.

12. What we believe about the future shapes how we live today. Our hope of resurrection should give us courage to follow Jesus, proclaiming the gospel with joy even when that involves suffering. Our ultimate descent to the grave leads on to glory with Christ.

NOTES

1. Garland, 429.
2. Garland, 436.
3. Garland, 448.
4. Garland, 449.
5. Garland, 454.

1. For example, we can be honest with God and ourselves about our desires and seek to align our desires with God's desires. We can ask ourselves, "What drives me? What are the motives behind what I'm doing now?" We can then seek to align our motives with God's. We can choose to look at things God wants us to pay attention to and not at things he sees as trivial (consider television). We can take the trouble to think about current events and ask what opinions God would want us to have. We can invest energy and money into things God wants done in the world.

2. Nearly all of us have a family member, neighbor, or coworker who is hard to love. Also, it may be hard for us to take the time and effort to care for strangers in need. Despite the emotional impact these people may have on us, we must try to see them as God sees them and to see ourselves as channels of God's grace and love to them.

3. To agree with Jesus without submitting to his authority is to remain the ruler of one's own life. Such a person denies that Jesus really is the Anointed One, the king. Saving faith is lived-out faith that Jesus is Lord of all.

4. It's impossible to submit to Jesus' authority without practicing his teaching about love. To submit to his authority involves submitting to a process of being trained to do the things he commanded, most of all to love others as we love ourselves. A new believer doesn't yet have the capacity to love as fully as Jesus asks us to love, but he commits himself to the Holy Spirit's training process.

5. Jesus denounces the teachers for dressing in ways that set them above others and presuming authority for themselves. Their clothing "expresses pride that hungers for honors and distinction."[1] They dress to impress. They crave status. They also disregard the poor (widows were often poor because they were vulnerable). They manipulate others out of their money. They practice religiosity for show.

6. The widow gives everything she has to God, making herself totally dependent on his care, with no need to impress others.

7. The disciples were likely shocked and appalled. But they believed Jesus and (probably with deep fear) wanted to know when it would happen.

8. Jesus predicts false messiahs, wars, earthquakes, and famines. He predicts that his disciples will be arrested, beaten, and tried as criminals, and that they will have a chance to witness before rulers. He predicts that families will be divided over faith in Christ, and that believers will be widely hated. What he tells his disciples to do when these things happen is to watch out to avoid deception, to not be afraid when wars and the like occur, to be on guard for arrest, to witness even when arrested, and to stand firm.

9. All of these bad things happened within the lifetimes of those disciples, and it has continued to happen. Wars, earthquakes, false prophets, family divisions, and persecutions have happened throughout Christian history. It's not clear that things are worse now than they were centuries ago; we are more aware of the global scale of evil because of our technology.

10. Jesus cares deeply about people. He cares that we suffer. He cares about people far more than great architecture, and because of the ultimate sacrifice he was about to make on the cross, the temple in Jerusalem would no longer be needed.

11. Jesus warns his followers against complacency, in whatever ways that might be expressed. Being consistently prayerful is one aspect of being on guard. Knowing the Scriptures so that we're not misled by false teachers is also important, as is pursuing growth in love for others. Jesus warns us over and over against spiritual laziness.

12. Predicting makes us feel we have some control. It helps some people manage anxiety about their lives. But it's far more valuable to put that energy into prayer and love for God and neighbor. God is worthy of our trust as we look to an unknown future.

NOTE

1. Garland, 479.

1. Jesus is anointed by a woman in the home of a former leper. This is about as low-status an anointing as a king could get. And this king will reign not on a throne but from a cross, so his anointing points not to triumph but to burial. It was customary to give to the poor on holy days, but Jesus wryly points out that the rabbis also see burying the dead as a good deed.

2. The woman's devotion contrasts starkly with Judas's betrayal. Her adoration contrasts with the chief priests' malice. She does far better than anything Jesus' male disciples do for him, while Judas does much worse than the rest.

3. Jesus knows that the man with the water jar will have a room they can use. (This may be a plan Jesus has arranged, as normally women fetched water, but we can't be sure.) He knows Judas will betray him. He knows he won't drink wine again until he drinks new wine in God's kingdom. He knows his disciples will all scatter when he is arrested. He knows Peter will disown him three times. He knows that after he rises from the dead he will lead the way to Galilee. Jesus' foreknowledge shows not only his divine nature but also that his sacrifice was voluntary and not a tragic misfortune.

4. The disciples are "saddened" (14:19) to learn there's a traitor in their midst. In fact, they are horrified. And none but Peter seems to be confident that they aren't the one, as they all ask, "Surely not I?" Peter is full of bravado, but it is misplaced because he doesn't know himself.

5. Jesus takes bread and, after giving thanks in the traditional Jewish manner, breaks it and gives it to his followers. Mark frames these scenes with parallel words so that we see that Jesus' whole mission has involved this same self-giving.

6. "[T]he Lord's Supper is not a memorial of something past and gone but reminds us of what the Lord has done for us and makes his death and his presence a living reality.... '[R]emembering' in the biblical idiom 'is not to entertain a pallid idea of a past event in one's mind, but to make the event present again so that it controls the will and becomes potent in our lives for good or ill.' The Lord's Supper reminds us who we are, what our story is, what our values are, and who claims us as his own."[1] Jesus gives

us himself as the food of eternal life. He makes us part of a covenant with God, sealed by his blood.

7. Jesus suffered not just physically but also emotionally. He was fully human and felt the full range of human emotions, including the anxiety of waiting and the desire to avoid suffering if at all possible. He wasn't eagerly charging toward martyrdom; he was heroically preparing himself to face the horror that was coming because he trusted his Father's will. No other Jew would have called God "Abba," the respectful but deeply intimate way Jews spoke to their human fathers. Jesus didn't hesitate to tell his Abba what he felt and what he longed for, yet he remained committed to his Abba's will. Death isn't something any human should eagerly seek. Death, and every deep distress, is something to be faced and mastered with intense and honest prayer. Jesus knew that his Father could do anything and was confident that even his painful will could be trusted.

8. Mark 14:38 implies that had the disciples watched and prayed as instructed, they might not have fallen when tempted to abandon Jesus. Praying in a crisis is good, but preparing for crisis through consistent prayer is even more important. We sometimes fail to pray because we don't know we're in a trial or about to be in one. "Sleeping" spiritually makes us unable to recognize that we are being tried, or unable to recognize a trial as God's will and to respond accordingly. Unprepared, the disciples fled.

9. Had Peter watched and prayed, he might not have fallen when he was tempted to deny Jesus. In his bravado, Peter had taken for granted the willingness of his spirit, and hadn't believed his flesh was weak.

10. Mark implies that Jesus was strengthened through prayer to endure the trial before him. By sandwiching Jesus' trial between two pieces of the story of Peter's failure, Mark suggests that we should compare Peter's and Jesus' response to persecution. Jesus remains silent when there's no point in speaking about the trumped-up charges, and then he makes the declaration that he knows will get him killed. He mastered his emotions by taking them to God, so he's completely in control of himself in the worst of circumstances. Prayer strengthened his trust in his Father's control of the circumstances he was in.

11. In the first half of Mark's gospel, Jesus continually displayed divine power: healing the sick, defeating demons, proving he had authority to forgive

the paralytic's sins. Had the Jerusalem leaders paid attention and sought to learn more, they might, like the disciples, have seen Jesus calm a storm, feed multitudes, and walk on water. But now at the end of Mark's story, Jesus is no longer displaying the flashy power. He is demonstrating that God reveals his ultimate power in weakness, in servanthood, in the willingness to take human suffering into himself. "All these leaders can see now is a rustic from Galilee, who was easily captured when one of his own followers betrayed him.... To imagine this man as God's Messiah, let alone as the one who exercises the power of God, must have seemed laughable to them if it were not so offensive."[2] When they taunt him to prophesy (14:65), they apparently forget that in 12:1–12 he prophesied they would kill him.

12. Mark has emphasized the disciples' thickheadedness throughout his gospel. They followed Jesus hoping for glory, and they fled when faithfulness got dangerous. Thirty or forty years later when Mark writes his gospel, Peter is a hero to younger Christians, but Mark makes a point of showing that Peter wasn't always a hero. (Peter very likely is the source of Mark's information, a transformed man who tells of his own weakness in order to help others.) Had the mission depended on Peter, or on anyone else other than Jesus, it would have failed. Disciples are deeply flawed, and the only reason the church's mission succeeds is because of Jesus' power working through the Holy Spirit.

NOTES

1. A. M. Hunter, *Jesus: Lord and Savior* (Grand Rapids: Eerdmans, 1976), 140, quoted in Garland, 534.
2. Garland, 564.

SESSION 12 LEADER'S NOTES

1. The chief priests have gathered and worked up a crowd to put pressure on Pilate. In order to free Jesus, Pilate would have to stand up to their political pressure and take the risk of a riot. Pilate has no moral backbone and will do whatever he can to satisfy the public. He doesn't care about truth or justice; he cares about comfort and keeping the peace. He will follow the easiest path.

   Today, many people attend church but avoid taking moral stances, especially public ones that will win them ridicule. Many politicians do what polls tell them is expedient, not what they know is right. It's hard for many Christians to come together to help victims of injustice in our country or around the world when we're preoccupied with managing our own households. We're busy people with a lot on our plates, but are we also morally indifferent?

2. Perhaps the chief priests would only have had to point out how Jesus has disappointed the crowds who hailed him as liberator when he rode into the city a few days earlier. The crowd wants a man of power as they understand power, someone who takes violent action against oppressors. "The choice of Barabbas represents the human preference for the one who represents our narrow personal hopes — in this particular case, a perverted nationalism. He appeals to our basic instinct to protect our interests, with violence if necessary."[1]

3. "[W]e have been indoctrinated to prefer the violent answer over the peaceful one.... We are more comfortable with the violent machismo of the knight-errant than with the passive suffering of a seemingly powerless savior who submits to beatings and mockery."[2] However, "Barabbas's way only doles out more violence in a never-ending cycle. Jesus' way soaks up the injustice, evil, and oppression like the venom of a sting and unleashes a far more powerful force of love and forgiveness. God's way responds to evil redemptively and short-circuits it. On the cross, Jesus took the sting of death and absorbed all the poison. Our failure to choose this way stems from our failure to trust God. We may trust God to take care of the afterlife, but we do not trust God enough to let go of too much control of the here and now. If we have to suffer, we would rather put our trust in the

Barabbases of this world, who fight back and murder enemies. We have yet to see that this way only leads to more death and tragedy."[3]

4. "Were he to save himself, he could not save others from something more deadly than storms or illnesses. The nails do not hold him fast to the cross; the love of God constrains him. He himself taught that whoever wants to save his own life will ultimately lose it (8:35). His detractors cannot understand this way of looking at life. They cannot see that he dies as a ransom for many (10:45) or that his body is being broken and his blood is poured out for the many (14:22–25)."[4] "God's power absorbs the toxin of human sin and hatred and turns it into salvation for all who put their trust in a God who loves this much and who works in this way. The gospel is the only thing that makes sense of a world so ugly and so beautiful."[5]

5. Jesus' garments are divided (Mark 15:24; Ps. 22:18). Robbers and villains encircle him; his hands and feet are pierced (Mark 15:27; Ps. 22:16). Mockers shake their heads at him (Mark 15:29; Ps. 22:7). They goad him to save himself (Mark 15:30–31; Ps. 22:8). They revile him (Mark 15:32; Ps. 22:6). He cries out in the anguish of forsakenness (Mark 15:34; Ps. 22:1, 11, 19–21). But the psalm ends with expectation that the Gentiles will worship God (Ps. 22:27; see Mark 15:39); God is king (Ps. 22:28); the sufferer will rise from death (Ps. 22:29–30); and future generations will proclaim his righteousness (Ps. 22:30–31).

6. We too can vent our feelings and complaints to God, realizing that he knows them anyway, and trust that he responds to our cry. We don't have to be afraid that God will reject us if we tell him what we feel. We can also refuse to give up on God even when we're overcome with terrible grief, when we feel utterly forsaken, or when it looks like good is defeated. We can pray, give fearless testimony, and endure taunts.

7. We can be confident that there is no barrier between God and us. God can get to us, and our prayers get to him. Jesus is the final sacrifice who bought our reconciliation with God.

8. Victims of crucifixion usually died slowly by suffocation as they grew weaker and couldn't raise their torsos up to breathe. The process often took days. Jesus died in a few hours, yet at the end he had enough strength for a loud cry (15:37). The centurion would have known how unusual this was. Perhaps the darkness over the land also moved him. Perhaps he was

touched by Jesus' self-mastery amid torture and taunts. "The cross reveals that God's love and power can win those one might never have dreamed would respond. The actions of the centurion who put Jesus to death and of Joseph, the respected and wealthy council member who condemned Jesus to death, mean that one can never write off an enemy. The power of the gospel is so great that even those who persecute Christians may be won to the faith."[6]

9. The cross tells us that God reveals his power most fully in his defeat of human sin through weakness. God can turn even mockery into a proclamation of the gospel. The cross reveals God's incredible love, what he is willing to go through for us.

10. We should believe the angel's message because, like these women, we have been on a journey following Jesus from his baptism in the Jordan through his ministry in Galilee, including his predictions of what would happen, and his fulfillment of the Old Testament Scriptures in the way he died. We should believe the angel's message because the women and Peter and the other disciples eventually did have the courage to go and tell that they had seen the risen Jesus, and many of them were martyred for refusing to deny what they knew they had seen. Mark doesn't offer us scientific proof of the resurrection. "If any want to see Jesus for themselves, they must leave the tomb and go where he leads — to Galilee, back to the beginning, where one must learn to follow him again. If we ask where the Christ is, Mark's answer is that he is always on ahead of us, leading us on to new lands. Jesus is to be found today in obedience to his command."[7]

11. The disciples' fear may be awe in the presence of God's powerful action. Or they could be afraid of what they don't understand. Like many devout Jews of that time, they believe that righteous people will rise at the end of the age (cf. John 11:24), but nothing (other than Jesus' promise) has prepared them for a man who rises from the dead here and now. Jesus' disciples have been slow to understand him all along, so it's not surprising that they're slow to grasp his greatest miracle. We, too, may be afraid to tell what we've been told about his resurrection, fearing that others will ridicule us for believing something so far-fetched.

NOTES

1. Garland, 583.
2. Ibid.
3. Ibid.
4. Garland, 591.
5. Garland, 606.
6. Garland, 607.
7. Garland, 624.